Cy (

Our Time is Now:

Six Essays on the Need for Reawakening

About the author

Cy Grant, ex RAF Flight Lieutenant, WWII, is well known as an actor and singer. He is also a qualified barrister, writer and cultural activist. Chairman of Drum Arts centre in the 1970s and Director of Concord Multicultural Festivals in the 1980s, he went on to become a member of the Scientific and Medical Network and is an Honorary Fellow of the University of Surrey, Roehampton.

Also by Cy Grant

Books

Black Words: Poems. Self Published c.1972
Ring of Steel: Pan Sound and Symbol. London: Macmillan Caribbean, 1999
A member of the RAF of Indeterminate Race: WWII experiences of a former POW. Woodfield Publishing, 2006
Blackness & the Dreaming Soul: Race Identity and the Materialistic Paradigm. Edinburgh: Shoving Leopard, 2007
Rivers of Time, the collected poems of Cy Grant. London: Naked Light, 2008

Radio Programmes

The Way of Nature. BBC World Service, 1980/1 (6 programmes)
Panning for Gold. BBC Radio 2, 1995 (2 programmes)

Cy Grant

Our Time is Now:

Six Essays on the Need for Reawakening

Edited and Introduced
by Ian Dieffenthaller

Cane Arrow Press

First published 2010 by
Cane Arrow Press
PO Box 219
Royston
SG8 1AZ

Selection & Introduction © Ian Dieffenthaller 2010
A CIP catalogue record is available from the British Library

ISBN 978-0-9562901-2-0

Cover photo of NGC 4414 courtesy Hubble Heritage Team/ AURA/ STScI / NASA
Photo of the author courtesy Walter Langille, son of Squadron Leader Alton Langille,
his Lancaster bomber pilot during WWII.

Printed by Imprint Academic

ACKNOWLEDGEMENTS

Acknowledgements are due to the editors of the following publications and websites where versions of these essays first appeared:

Scientific & Medical Network Network Review
Itz Caribbean website
Blackness & the Dreaming Soul, Shoving Leopard
Ring of Steel, Macmillan Caribbean

Thanks also to Terrence Brathwaite, Sr. Lecturer in Comparative Law at Coventry University for suggesting the link between Legba and Lt Green in the essay *Deciphering Hidden Codes &Synchronicities: Coincidence & Meaning.*

Both Anne Baring, the writer, lecturer and Jungian analyst and David Lorimer of the Scientific and Medical Network have been extremely supportive in this latest phase of my writing, for which I give thanks.

This book
is dedicated to all involved in the
Manifesto for Change,
the New Renaissance of Consciousness
already astir in the synthesis
of Science
and the
Dreaming Soul

Thank God our time is now when wrong
Comes up to face us everywhere,
Never to leave us till we take
The longest stride of soul men ever took.
Affairs are now soul size.
The enterprise
is exploration into God.
Where are you making for? It takes
So many thousand years to wake
But will you wake for pity's sake?

Christopher Fry: A Sleep of Prisoners

CONTENTS

INTRODUCTION

I first came across Cy Grant's writing via a lone poem in John Figueroa's second *Caribbean Voices* anthology of 1970. It was not until I began my research into West Indian poetry in Britain two decades later that I finally met the man. That meeting came about through a mutual interest in the steel pan of Trinidad and Tobago rather than via poetry but we both agree that there isn't much to choose between the two – they both come out of a fascinating hybrid culture. Cy was giving an audio-visual presentation at the University of Birmingham, occasioned by the publication of *Ring of Steel*, his book on the evolution of pan. It soon became clear to us both that the underlying theme of that book was the struggle, not just of an instrument but of a people out of colonial subjugation and into worldwide acceptance. It also contained the germ of all of Cy's subsequent writing which has been directed at the ills of the post-colonial western worldview which seems to cause us to drift further from our basic humanity every day.

Cy's next book, *Blackness & the Dreaming Soul*, was a hybrid creature, beginning as an autobiography and becoming a philosophical tract on the hubris of society and what might be done to counter this. Now in his ninety-first year, Cy has had the dubious pleasure of witnessing at first hand, the end of empire, the emergence and decline of the iron curtain and the headlong plunge into dualism – the cult of 'us and them'. As a West Indian who has lived for half a century in Britain, fought and been shot down for the mother country and come to us via both acting and the law, he is ideally placed to comment on modern times. His style, while often plain speaking is underwritten by a poetic sensibility, for Cy has written and read poetry for over seventy years; his authoritative yet meditative tone is based on decades of attention to wise men from all walks of life – from the master Lao Tzu to Nelson Mandela.

This short volume of essays splits roughly into two sections. At first, the author explores the current direction of western society and its failure to acknowledge the root of its basic tenets. This leads to the notion of 'West is Best', the desire for world dominance and the restless attempts to assimilate the rest of the world's peoples to the prevailing worldview. Having looked at the status quo, we return to our old favourite, pan, as the fundamental symbol for cosmic repair. The essay 'Pan as Cosmic Symbol' starts the search for a new consciousness – acknowledging that the hermetic tradition of alchemy embedded in the manufacture and unique sound qualities of the instrument had its roots in Africa, home of our most recent common ancestor, or 'Mitochodrial Eve'. The last two essays set out Cy's concept of a new dream, a quest for that new consciousness embedded in the wisdom of the ancients. If we call to mind Plato's Allegory of the Cave, the author's notion is that we are like Plato's prisoners, our worldview confined to understanding the shadows within. We are prisoners of scientific empiricism, trapped in a latter day cave of illusion. But unlike Plato's captives, we do have a choice to awaken to a new consciousness of who and what we really are.

With the author's permission, I have presented the essays in the order that seemed to me to flow naturally, rather than accordingly to absolute chronology. There have been revisions since the pieces were first published but I have resisted the temptation to edit out all repetition as to do so might have damaged the structure of the text and removed the true sense of the original context; I would ask the reader to accept this as reiteration rather than remissness.

One of the themes that weaves through all the texts is that of the ancient wisdom of the Tao te Ching and African animism, which might be employed to redress the imbalances within contemporary 'black' culture, the direct descendant of the post-WWII neocolonialism faced by the West Indian in Britain. Another surrounds the increasing fragmentation of a left-brain orientated society, the product of scientific empirical endeavour yet capable of being righted by the new ways of seeing made possible by the 'new physics'. In 1945, the author wrote the following poem as a POW:

> The world revolves
> but time stands still;
> distant memories…
> laughter, hurry John we'll miss the fun.
> Desiree, you are so soft, I love you;
> the city clock booming the hour
> hurrying faces, kiosks… a stranger's smile
> What's the matter, son?
> I slipped on barbed wire, Dad
> Barbed wire? Let me see,
> there, it's not too bad,
> it will not hurt within the hour…
>
> the world revolving
> time standing still…
> there's an awful stench in this room.
>
> On three-tiered bunks we lie,
> prisoners
> staring with vacant eye.

Five decades on, the world is still at war. The old lie, 'it will not hurt…' still flourishes. We still will not see reality. What differs from this wartime vignette is that the world is now spinning out of control as we race against time in the ultimate combat. These essays suggest how easy it is to reconnect science with soul and to rely once more on ancient truths that cannot be named or owned, merely experienced. And in this spirit, the last essay both sums up and provides us with a point of departure.

Ian Dieffenthaller, December 2009

1. The Way of the West

Originally published in *Scientific & Medical Network Review*, Summer 2008

A Wake-up Call

The fundamental message of my book, *Blackness & the Dreaming Soul*, is a plea for the West to wake; a plea for a reconstruction of the way in which we make our reality. The way of the West, it seems to me, is not the way of Nature, but a self-seeking, consumer-orientated global cultural juggernaut that spells disaster for our beautiful planet Earth and for all life on it. The question I'm forced to ask is why, with all the evidence before us, we remain trapped in cultural hubris; why we cannot mobilise to avert the ecological holocaust that threatens our very survival. Why don't we make that shift in consciousness that would transform our degraded world? Why not avoid division and war against each other and against our very home, making that home a better place for all mankind?

We seem to be caught up in a race against time; caught in a dualism: instead of seeking balance in all things, competition and greed motivates and divides us.

Whilst racism has little to do with my brief, it has been the catalyst that has forced me to try to make sense of my worlds. I believe in the essential goodness and oneness of mankind, a belief that has been so little shared and explored that it seems almost impossible for us to see ourselves for what we truly are, as an integral part of the mystery of life, capable of viewing our home, our unique place in the Universe as sacred – the only planet as far as we know, with a delicate and fragile life support system, floating in the incomprehensible magnitude of space – a spherical garden of such beauty and wonder.

Despite our science, our burgeoning technologies, our welfare state, the accessibility of university education for all our exploits into outer space and wonderful achievements in every field of endeavour, our very existence, it seems, is threatened. We have continual warfare with the collateral damage and human suffering that results; nuclear and other weapons of mass destruction; star wars; satellite surveillance systems. Nuclear waste debris orbits the fragile atmosphere of our planet; we hear talk of global warming – carbon and radiation footprints, depletion of natural resources – deforestation, pollution of our seas, fuel shortages, genocide, drug abuse, rape, child abuse, sex slavery, racism, ...the list goes on and on.... And we still pride ourselves that our way of life is best.

Carl Jung, a student of alchemy suggested 'that the generally accepted Western world view based on rationalism is not the only possible one and is not all embracing, but in many ways a prejudice and a bias that ought perhaps to be corrected'. He believed that modern man had not truly looked into the great divide within, which separated him from wilderness and nature. In a worldview based on this reality, we strive for more and more technological advances that will prolong our lives but do not ensure the same for our children and future generations. How selfish can we be? The old patterns repeat themselves. In Medicine we produce more drugs with disastrous side effects. We put our trust in gene therapy and genetic engineering; genetically modified food instead of organic; agricultural seed patents and now bio-fuel. We ban cigarettes but have longer drinking hours, more gaming houses, more things to distract us; to fill the void, more bargains, more sex, more fame and are rewarded by more crime; we talk of zero tolerance but do not address the issues responsible for the disillusionment that feeds it; so opt for more prisons, more policemen. We know about the carbon footprint yet build more terminals (how appropriate) leading to more air miles, more pollution, spiralling debts, an unstable economy, celluloid violence, toys, play stations and other excesses.

'More' is the daily mantra which we materialise and export – globalisation, colonisation of other cultures – monoculture and over-production to satisfy our every whim. In turn the newly colonised abandon their traditions and cater to our needs with their fakes and their quick fixes thus exacerbating the pollution and the degradation.

A Return to Native Value

People of the African diaspora suffered tremendously from colonisation of the mind. They are still unable to disentangle themselves from the identity of 'collective victim', rooted in the memory of slavery, which falsely gives them a sense of solidarity – a position that engenders further rejection, one which I call the 'black trap'. This reality can only be transmuted by the knowledge of who these people really are, thus making themselves able to contribute positively to the healing of society. Indeed, their mere presence is already doing just that – making Europe confront its racism. Worldwide, Martin Luther King and Nelson Mandela have shown that they can influence and change entrenched attitudes. Mandela was once considered a terrorist. My particular hero has been Aimé Césaire, the great revolutionary politician, poet and philosopher from Martinique who died recently. His revolt against Europe is what worked on me in a subliminal yet positive way. It wasn't just a revolt against racism, colonialism and the excesses of European culture but a call for a return to our native human values, to recognize that Nature is alive and bounteous and that we should not abuse her. If we do, we abuse ourselves, our very home. Black people still aspire to be accepted. They revolt rightly against injustice but still seek to integrate with the perpetrators of injustice and the gatekeepers of civilisation.

In the English speaking world black people are generally unaware of the contribution of Césaire. Frantz Fanon, author of the

Wretched of the Earth – the bible of the Black Power movement in 1960s America – acknowledges Césaire as his mentor. The exponents of black power knew about 'Black is Beautiful', but alas only on a superficial level. Césaire's plea was for a reconnection with the natural and a call for the emergence of a new man. The black press in Britain, I am told, did not even carry an obituary of the great man. That's how ignorant we are – unaware of our roots in Mother Africa, home of the Mitochondrial Eve[1]; and Egypt where Pythagoras, the presiding genius of European culture studied for two decades; unaware that Pythagoras' teachings were based on Egyptian (and so African) mathematical and religious pantheistic principles.

Despite the West's great 'civilisation' we live in fear fanned by those who seek control, or profit (without our consumer society our whole financial structure would collapse); fear of one another, the outsider, the terrorist. We defend our 'values' at all costs – all others must conform. Each fear is symptomatic of the underlying degraded state of the present age. In *Blackness and the Dreaming Soul* I explore the causes of our current alienation from the natural, primordial world, and ourselves, unearthing the darkness of the human psyche. It is an attempt to understand how we've come to such an impasse. Out of concern for the direction in which we seem to be heading, it is written hopefully – to shed light on our mutual plight, on the dehumanised, self-destructing and violent world in which we find ourselves. It aims not to be bitter or recriminatory and is offered not just as negative criticism, for such criticism only invites polarisation.

---

[1] Mitochondrial DNA [mtDNA] is extranuclear and survives outside the core of the cells of our bodies. It is unaffected by the usual genetic mixing of our parents, mutating only slowly over centuries. Passed down the female line, it has been traced back to our *most recent common ancestor*, our 'Mitochondrial Eve', located on the African continent some 200,000 years ago.

An Inconvenient Truth

Al Gore's *An Inconvenient Truth*[2] laments the global crisis facing mankind but does not propose a solution. It is true that we have the know-how to deal with the problem but somehow we do not use it. The inconvenient truth is that the outer environment reflects the inner. There must be a change in the mindset. If we hope to bring about change we must first change within. This holds true for the individual as well as for society. What may appear to be essentially a critique of the prevailing Western social, political, economic and globalised industrial system is rather a plea for a fundamental change in the way we make our reality and so, in human consciousness. The Western system of secular consumerism perpetuates itself through its greed, its multinational corporations, its educational institutions and the media.

I was brought up in this system, yet destined to remain outside it, a black man caught up in a white culture, the great grandson of a slave, indoctrinated by an English education, a volunteer in the Royal Air Force in World War II, commissioned as an Officer, shot down and a prisoner of war in Nazi Germany for two years. On discharge, I qualified as a Barrister only then to become fully aware that I was an indeed an outsider – no place for black lawyers in the 1950s. My only choice, it seemed at the time, was to become an actor on the stage of life and also a singer, not without some success. But it was a fickle success. Enoch Powell saw to that. As a cultural activist I set up the first Black arts centre in London in the 1970s only to realise that this was creating even more separation. I was rescued by Aimé Césaire. I toured his epic redemptive poem *Cahier d'un Retour au pays natal* (Return to My Native Land) for two years in theatres around Britain. This led to me setting up Concord Multicultural Arts Festivals in the 1980s, to

---

[2] *An Inconvenient Truth: The Planetary Emergency of Global Warming and What We Can Do About it*. London: Bloomsbury, 2006.

promote the cultural diversity of present day Britain – a plea for
unity in diversity – a plea largely ignored at the time and still not
understood today. In my search for identity, meaning and a sense of
belonging, I still found myself marginalized all along the way so I
was forced to explore what was wrong with this culture in which I
was bred and brought up.

I began writing *Blackness & the Dreaming Soul* as an attempt
to record my outer journey but as fate would have it, it became my
inner journey of self-discovery and healing. We inherit the systems
of our forebears, our culture, so there is no blame here. My book is, I
hope, an honest reappraisal of how we make our way in life and an
appeal for healing of society and our fragmented and endangered
world. We need to reverse the prevailing all-pervasive primacy of
mind over Nature. Science and empiricism have been entrenched
too long as the ruling principles – an existential reality, the creation
of our minds and intellect, unaware of our deeper connection to the
earth itself, to Mother Nature and to our true being, who and what
we really are – the primordial wisdom of the mystery of life, but
first we have to make that descent into the darkness in order to
transcend the dominance of the intellect.

The Primacy of Science

The primacy of mind assumes that Science will solve all our
problems. A prominent scientist recently claimed on TV that as
Master of the Universe, he hopes one day to discover that over-
arching 'Theory of Everything' that will answer all our questions
about the nature of reality and so solve all our problems; this, whilst
claiming that our destiny lies somewhere out there in space. We are
already out there in space! This misconception is typical of the
delusion of yet another prominent scientist, that Science will
confirm that selfishness is the norm of Nature (survival of the
fittest) and that there is obviously no place for co-operation or

symbiosis – no place for the existence of a higher intelligence, an absurd position for a University professor responsible for the education of future generations. Science has replaced Wisdom. It has moved away from the beliefs of the founders of its own discipline – the philosopher/scientist, Aristotle, who saw Nature as one unified whole; Sir Isaac Newton, deeply religious and a practising alchemist. Today we demand empirical proof for everything but all we end up with is theories all of which can be disproved with the passage of time. Scientific theories follow one another in quick succession[3], yet Science still operates within clearly defined parameters of the orthodoxy of the moment; in other words a purely scientific paradigm resists paradigm change.

Science only investigates the physical, material nature of the universe and so only gets answers in mathematical terms – how many molecules, or genes there are in cells, for instance. It cannot explain how information jumps the synapses in the brain, or how something can be both a wave and a particle at the same time even when it can observe these phenomena.

Science cannot explain how the information stored in a single cell of DNA is of a magnitude comparable with that stored in a tiny acorn that grows into a massive oak tree; or the extensive abilities in art and in mathematics of children with autism or Savant syndrome like Stephen Wiltshire, despite obvious neurological abnormalities that are found in the left hemispheres of their brains. We surely should be able to deduce that our survival as a species does not depend on rationalism, on our minds alone, or on ruthless competition and control of nature but in living in harmony with nature and one another.

Some of the most important scientific discoveries have been made when the mind is no longer focused purely on solving the problem. Suddenly the solution *mysteriously* surfaces. This was the

---

[3] See the discussion on p137 of Holons and Holograms in *Blackness & the Dreaming Soul*.

case with Newton and the falling apple; Einstein day dreaming in a tram as it approached another (relativity); James Watson riding a bicycle having viewed – and then appropriated – Rosalind Franklin's radio photographic work (the DNA double helix); and the dream of August Kekulé which led to the development of organic chemistry. Kekulé saw a snake dancing and biting its own tail, a vision which led to his discovery of the molecular structure of benzene. He interpreted his dream to mean that the structure was a closed carbon ring and fundamental to organic chemistry.[4]

Scientific enquiry is the orthodoxy – the yardstick on which we base our reality, our sense of being, and our future. This is the fundamental flaw. We do not know who or what we are, yet think that we can discover this by our minds alone, only a fraction of which we use in any case. Had the notion of the primacy of Nature prevailed we would not be in the mess we are today. We would fight with all our might to preserve our unique home, Mother Earth, which depends on a very delicate atmospheric balance that supports all life and which provides us with everything we need for our survival. We defend our little homes, our countries or cultures, but miss the whole picture – our home is Mother Earth, Mother Nature.

Everything is Enfolded in Everything Else

The indigenous peoples of the Earth knew by intuition that everything is interconnected. But modern man has abandoned this inner knowledge in favour of empirical proof, something that the New Physics[5] so clearly demonstrates as impossible. The observer influences what he observes: there can be no empirical proof! Yet

---

[4] August Kekulé, *Textbook of organic chemistry or the chemistry of the carbon compounds, etc.* Erlangen, 1861.
[5] Much has been written recently but see for instance Gordon Fraser's *The New Physics*.

we ignore the philosophical and existential implications of quantum reality. The theoretical physicist, David Bohm[6] has provided us with a holographic model in which life and inanimate matter are not separate. For Max Planck one of the founders of Quantum Mechanics[7], 'matter' implied a bundle of energy which is given form by an intelligent spirit. The Fractal Geometry of the French mathematician, Benoit Mandelbrot[8] comes to the same conclusion – that every thing is enfolded in every thing else, similar to that of the French experimental physicist Alain Aspect[9], that there is an unbroken wholeness or interconnectedness in the Universe. Also there is the new worldview of the transpersonal psychologist, Stanislav Grof,[10] that there are *no absolute boundaries between body/ego and the totality of existence...*

Despite the recent outstanding developments in nanotechnology, we are still stuck in outdated concepts. Our present explosion in technological knowledge clearly demonstrates that there was (and still is) so much out there of which we were (and still are) unaware by our reliance only on the power of the intellect. If we see that what is *out there* is also our innermost being, we will then know who we truly are and so re-connect to that wisdom beyond description; beyond the duality that divides and bedevils us.

Throughout the ages we have witnessed the indomitable spirit of man, that we have produced great music and great art and are capable of the noblest deeds, the greatest compassion, bravery and achievement, all attributes that stem, not from the intellect, the

---

[6] David Bohm, *Wholeness & the Implicate Order.*

[7] Max Planck – the originator of wave/particle duality based on the overtone series in music in which notes jump from whole number to whole number – deduced that *particle energy in the atom changes not gradually but in jumps.*

[8] Benoit Mandelbrot, *Fractal Geometry.*

[9] Alain Aspect's *non-locality*

[10] Stanislav Grof, *Holotrophic Breath.*

rational, but from a deeper source, our true natures – the wisdom of our bodies – our autonomous systems and our breath, the umbilical chord that connects us all, all races and all life on our planet to our Mother – Primordial Nature.

2. BEYOND THE JARGON: REDEFINING
MULTICULTURALISM

This essay was originally presented in 2004 to CRONEM (Centre for Research on Nationalism, Ethnicity and Multiculturalism) at their inaugural Summer Conference at the University of Surrey.

Introduction

In accepting CRONEM's invitation to give this paper on the Future of Multiculturalism in Europe I am aware that my contribution raises questions that go beyond a purely academic remit, in an attempt to get to the heart of a Western ideology that seems to have less and less space for such topics.

I am very happy to note, however, that CRONEM's policy statement makes it quite clear that a multi-disciplinary approach would be adopted in its research. I am interpreting this to mean that not only will all faculties of the academy be called upon to contribute to the discussions but that global perspectives will also be brought to bear on them. We live in a multicultural world, which constitutes the very basis of human evolution and existence. Implicit in this is the need to take into account how other peoples in the world interpret their realities; in other words, the adoption of an holistic approach.

I have always been concerned about the fragmentation that bedevils all of our systems of learning and epistemology. I am especially so these days with the breaking up of scientific knowledge into its constituent parts, so that what should enhance our perception actually obscures our view of the fundamental interconnectedness of all things. This, as you will hear, is my main proposition; and something, I believe, that should form part of our deliberations.

As a West Indian in Britain, I believe that I speak from the liminal space of outsider with more inside knowledge than most, and I ask your indulgence whilst I give a brief account of my own journey through the minefield, or should I say, the mind field, associated with migration, ethnicity and multiculturalism.

I was born in a British colony, British Guiana, and came to Britain in 1941, not as an immigrant, but as a volunteer to fight Nazism. In fact the first major influx of so-called immigrants from the West Indies in the last century, came by invitation, to join His Majesty's Services during World War II. They were even encouraged to join the Royal Air Force, something that would have been quite impossible a year before. I flew with the RAF as an officer in a Lancaster bomber, was shot down in 1943 and spent two years in a prisoner of war camp in Germany.

The most significant number of immigrants from the West Indies, however, came here after the war, in the period known as the 'Windrush era' in recollection of the June 1948 docking of the SS Empire Windrush at Tilbury. The ship, with almost 500 West Indians aboard, was the first of three such ships to come to Britain in 1948 alone. Those West Indians had come at the invitation of the British Government to take up jobs that Britain desperately needed filling. At the time of their arrival I was a law student at the Middle Temple. But it was only when I was called to the Bar in 1951 that questions of ethnic identity began to be a problem for me personally. By ethnic identity I mean race. I found it impossible to find Chambers or any form of work; and so I was forced, or so it seemed to me at the time, to go into show business as the only career I could pursue.

Since that time I have achieved limited success both as an actor and singer. I sang the news in calypso for the BBC's highly successful and innovative *Tonight* programme from 1957-1960, a highly charged era which saw the first race 'riots' in Britain erupt in

Notting Hill – the culmination of the racism that the new immigrants were experiencing. It was not surprising that along with the fan mail I was receiving, there was also the occasional hate mail. This put things into perspective for me. It was quite all right to be an entertainer or perhaps a sportsman, but quite another to be a barrister or indeed, a policeman. Things have changed somewhat since those days but there is still a long way to go.

Before my long stint on *Tonight* I had established quite a good career as an actor, not only on stage and TV but also in film. *Tonight* changed all that; I was seen as a calypso singer even though my repertoire consisted of songs from all over the world. Ironically, I had turned to singing as there were so few roles for black actors who faced the existential dilemma of playing only 'black' roles – ones that reflected their perceived status in society. The excuse given was that they did not have enough experience – a chicken and egg situation.

More than a decade later, things had got no better. Enoch Powell's 1968 'Rivers of Blood' speech, clearly endorsed the real state of public opinion. But it was to galvanize me into action. At the same time, the Civil Rights movement in America was in full swing and this was the necessary spur for me to revaluate how I would relate to the racism which I saw as endemic in European society; and which I suspect is like a shadow behind all our deliberations.

I decided to set up Drum, a black arts centre in 1974. 'Drum' was the title of a poem I had written about this time and was a symbol of the traditional healing power of African spirituality. The Centre was the first Black arts venue in the country and its specific purpose was to give black actors the necessary experience it was claimed they lacked and also to assert their search for identity. I had read somewhere that we would have to define ourselves or be defined. It was nothing to do with being separatist. In fact the case for a black theatre workshop rested on whether it was separatist to argue for a black consciousness. In an ideal world, concepts like race, nationality and ethnicity would be unimportant. To argue for an English cultural tradition as distinct from a French or American tradition would hardly be considered separatist: neither the National Theatre nor the Welsh Eisteddfod are seen as separatist or chauvinistic.

Drum was not an easy exercise. There had been a great deal of opposition from all quarters, notably the Arts Council of Great Britain. But in the end we won through, helped perhaps because I had become a household name during my days on the *Tonight* programme. Drum set up workshops for actors, exhibitions and poetry readings. One workshop led to the production of Mustapha Matura's play *Bread* at the Young Vic; and also to workshops at the National Theatre.

But I was soon to realise that defining myself solely as black, trapped within a white culture, was itself creating even more division.   This is a trap that even the justifiably angry and disillusioned black people, including academics, have found it difficult to break out of. It's no good just asserting one's blackness or the truth about Africa, the greatness of Egypt, Benin and Timbuktu and so exposing the blatant bias of western historiography. Divisiveness from whatever quarter separates us from each other and is the root cause of our present ecological and spiritual crisis.

Miraculously about this time, I had come across the great surreal poem *Cahier d'un Retour aux Pays Natal*, (Return to my Native Land), by the Martiniquan diplomat and poet, Aimé Césaire. At first reading it appears to be only about the deconstruction of colonialism and of asserting one's negritude, or blackness. Today the concept of negritude has lost its appeal as no longer historically relevant. Négritude, the movement, as Leopold Senghor conceived it, is largely discredited, and not just by the West. It has been seen as limited in its ideological, and political significance. But from my reading of the 'Cahier', as it is known, I saw it in a completely different and ultimately significant light – not just an oppositional concept of one system against another, however limited or justifiable that may be, but in fact, a universal concept that goes beyond secular academic theorizing with its specialized and fragmented tradition; it was a concept applicable to our divorce from nature and so for all peoples.

For me it was essentially a call for a rejection of purely Western materialistic values and of a return to ancient African values of community and a sense of total belonging. It gripped my imagination. I resigned from Drum and within a year began to tour the Cahier as a one-man performance throughout the country. This lasted for two and a half years, a significantly long association which indirectly introduced me to the ancient southern African concept of force which unifies the whole of creation, called *Modimo* – total participation with nature and of belonging.

Whilst touring, I also came across another book, this time from China – an ancient treatise, the Tao te Ching, by Lau Tzu. It too confirmed the sense of oneness with nature and has formed the basis of my outlook on life since then. And so it was, that when further race riots erupted again in the inner cities in the early 1980s, my answer was to set up Concord Multicultural Festivals, celebrating the cultural diversity of Britain at the time. Contrary to the way the arts are perceived in Europe, the arts of other cultures were not art for art's sake, but linked to life giving ceremonies and rites of passage. I thought that maybe we could learn from these other cultures.

Over a period of six years we staged festivals in seventeen cities throughout Britain and two countywide festivals. But what struck me most was that the media completely ignored this initiative even though the events were all staged in the most prestigious theatres in the major cities of England and were almost always very successful. This reinforced what I can now see as a thread that runs through all my life experiences as a black man in Britain – the marginalisation of one's status and one's dignity, and of any initiatives one may have to counter the situation. One was being forced to conform to the prevailing cultural norm.

Fortunately for me I had also developed a keen interest in the 'New Physics' – quantum mechanics, the philosophical implications of which seemed to challenge all orthodox views of reality. I had at last stumbled on a western scientific system which supported what Taoism and African animism were saying about the nature of reality – the interconnectedness of all things – and began to make sense of what I felt was wrong with the prevailing Western paradigm: a paradigm without a deep sense of meaning, of communality and respect for nature as it is not as we'd wish it to be. This realisation made me withdraw from society and eventually led to my writing about my experiences.

Soon the anger and frustration I had felt for most of my life began to be eroded. I began to see that things were not just what they appeared to be on the surface; that the empirical proof of Western Science itself was being challenged; that our historiography was blatantly biased. Bringing all these diverse ways of looking at reality (the New Physics, African belonging, Taoist non-duality) into a cohesive framework made me begin to further question our so-called civilisation. It seemed that the West was locked in a dualism that divorced it from Nature, that its only drive was to conquer nature; to control, to prescribe; to claim the moral high ground on all issues; that things get better if we have better technology; if we can manipulate our genes, if we can have more things regardless of the ecological cost. Everything was motivated by our rush to acquire more things than we need. The *being* [as opposed to *having*] mode was certainly not what a secular society was all about.

The Clubs of Rome and Budapest warn about the prospects of our survival beyond a couple of decades. Our vast intelligence is not ours in reality – we are only fractals of the Universal Intelligence that spawned us. It only adds to our hubris, instead of teaching us respect for our planet and each other.

Having been involved in multiculturalism in practice, I felt the need to redefine the notion itself. The term is an increasingly problematic one, both for those on the Clapham omnibus and for theorists in the academy. For many it is little more than the political expedient of an umbrella of peoples, co-existing by limited cultural exchange. For others, its ultimate purpose lies in the true cross-cultural model that can lead to new ways of perceiving ourselves and of learning from other cultures. Too often, the ideas imbedded in the term 'multiculturalism' are lost within the jargon surrounding theoretical constructions of ethnicity and hybridity. What we need to explore is the inter-culturality that does not exclude other cultures.

We have to define multiculturalism, but also what it is to be British. What we term Multiculturalism is in fact part of an expanding culture flowering out of a chequered history and providing a unique and relevant opportunity to show that it is more than a political expedient, and can be a model based on a spiritual understanding of the Universe. We need to cut across all conventional categories and realise the potential for unity in diversity not only in Britain, but also throughout the so-called 'civilized' world.

I believe that the core concern should be less about integration per se, and more to do with a vision/version of community beyond globalisation, in which all things are connected; man and nature, earth and cosmos; a notion curiously confirmed by recent scientific discoveries that human beings, animals and plants all share the same DNA code. The physicist David Bohm, in *Wholeness and the Implicate Order*, extrapolated this interconnectedness into what he called a 'holographic' view of the Universe, a view of which many scientists are also becoming aware. We, too, need to inculcate this interconnectedness in our outlook.

It seems that the West as a whole is driven by a rationality that destroys balance, that the duality inherent in any balanced system is replaced by a dualism that results only in elemental discord. This I have previously defined as The Seven Pillars of the Prevailing Paradigm that the West seeks to impose on the world thus polarising it into opposing camps. The events of the 11th of September 2001 exemplify this condition and were a defining moment in history. They point toward the need to rediscover and develop the ancient societal models mentioned above and which cut across all conventional categories in order to realise the potential for unity in diversity.

Our worldview creates our reality – how we perceive things. If we see division we get division. If we see our culture as the only one that matters we do not see the whole picture – that we live in a holistic world. This is what I had tried to challenge with the Concord festivals. In order to realise a world without fragmentation and confrontation, and to ensure the very survival of our planet and all species, we will require radical reconstruction of the way in which we make our reality; to first look out of Europe to ancient cultural practices which may inform our own situation and allow us to view multiculturalism in a new light and so reclaim the ability to go beyond meaningless, debatable categories.

What do we mean by culture? According to the *Shorter Oxford Dictionary*, 'it is the training and refinement of mind, tastes and manners; the condition of being thus trained and refined; the intellectual side of civilisation' – acquainting ourselves of the best that is known and said in the world; i.e, not only of Europe. For the *Penguin English Dictionary* it is a 'state of intellectual, artistic and social development of a group, type and degree of civilisation'.

The fact is that cultures are not static. They change or evolve as everything else in creation does. Similarly, ethnicity, as we know it, is socially produced. We need to challenge the idea that ethnic identity claims are inescapable and unequivocal, i.e. historically determined and irreversible. Just as there are not pure cultures, so there are no pure races biologically. In *Black Spark, White Fire*, Richard Poe, exposes 'the myth of the pure race' as proposed by so many champions of this Master Race theory, claiming that it violates not only the evidence of history, but 'one of the core principles of modern genetics' known as heterosis, proposed by Luigi Luca Cavalli-Sforza, Professor Emeritus of Human Genetics at Stanford University.   Cavalli-Sforza has been one of the most important figures in post-war studies of genetic diversity and the evolution of biological (or genetic) and cultural diversity in their most general sense. His theory is that 'when widely different gene pools are crossed – whether among people, plants, or animals – the hybrid offspring often turn out to be healthier, stronger, larger, or otherwise better developed than either parent', a phenomenon known as 'heterosis, or hybrid vigour'. His scientific refutations of racism go back a long way dismantling the determinist explanations for ethnically-based disparities in IQ scores, and suggesting that racist research should not be publicly funded. He shows that race and racism are destructive fallacies; and that what is needed is a multi-disciplinary approach to anthropology, and research that is collaborative on questions involving ethics, race, language and culture – in other words, an holistic approach. He believed that 'mixed marriages, including those between people of very different origins (incidentally, like my own and my parents before me and those of my own children), create a more robust line of descendants'.

Poe argues convincingly that when adapted to the domain of human psychology, this phenomenon may well have played the crucial role in the 'joining of the peoples of Europe, Africa and Asia in a melting pot of unusual size and richness' within the Mediterranean Basin, where Greece benefited most from Egypt. This African/Egyptian influence on Greece underpinned by the scientific fact that human beings 'need diversity to thrive' had led directly to the greatness of ancient Hellenic culture from which Europeans naively claim lineage, resulting in intellectual and technological prowess, but without acknowledging the Afro-Asiatic influence on Greece itself. But Poe is at pains to point out that it is not just biological heterosis, but a kind of heterosis of the mind that accounted for this phenomenon. 'The peoples of the Mediterranean traded cultures, religions and ideas' – a significant reason why so many civilizations flourished in the area whilst northern Europe was still uncivilized.

Poe cites the archaeologist and scholar of ancient languages and Near East Culture, Cyrus Gordon, whose interpretation of the phenomenon known as 'international stimulation,' proposes that 'all highly technologically developed civilizations are the result of international stimulation so that all of them are connected by what they have learned from each other.' Gordon held that 'cultural flowering' was the result of the melting pot of cultures. He believed that no people were pure, racially or linguistically: 'Creative peoples, and the languages they speak, are the results of felicitous combinations.'

I believe that this is what is taking place in Britain today. Historically, Britain has been conservative, resistant to change. But we live in a rapidly changing world. In the last two decades we have seen political barriers such as the Berlin wall and systems like the Communist world crumble. There is certainly no danger of anything so drastic taking place in Britain and there is no threat of cultural breakdown. Britain has shown that it can accommodate people from its old Commonwealth. According to the British historian, Arnold Toynbee, an essential element in cultural breakdown if it were to happen, would be a loss of flexibility. When social structures and behaviour patterns become so rigid that society cannot adapt to changing situations, society will be unable to carry on the creative process of cultural evolution. Although a cultural mainstream may become petrified by clinging to fixed ideas and rigid patterns of behaviour, 'creative minorities' will bring about a pattern of interaction leading to growth:

> 'The dominant social institutions will refuse to hand over their leading roles to these new cultural forces, but they will inevitably go on to decline and disintegrate, and the creative minorities may be able to

transform some of the old elements into a new configuration. The process of cultural evolution will then continue, but in new circumstances and with new protagonists.' (*A Study of History*).

The classic example of 'cultural evolution' occurs in Toynbee's own writing. His major work, *A Study of History* [twelve volumes over twenty-seven years] was structured according to the rise and fall of civilisations, and embodied his theory of historical progress. In it he stated that 'It will be seen that when we classify mankind by colour, the only primary race that has not made a creative contribution to any civilization is the Black Race'. Yet it was Toynbee who later claimed that: 'It may be the black man who will give the new spiritual dynamic to Western civilization that it so desperately needs to survive... the spiritual power... that comes from love, understanding, good will and non-violence', [Quoted in Stephen Oates, *Let the Trumpet Sound, a biography of Martin Luther King*] – ironically, a clear example of the creative process of cultural evolution.

Be that as it may, another form of accommodation can be seen if we consider how the Notting Hill Carnival has evolved over the past four decades. I'm not so sure that the word 'evolved' is the right one – it was more a case of social engineering. Although not against authority, Carnival, was opposed to indiscriminate authoritarianism, obeying its own inner convictions and collective knowledge, perpetuating its own life and its own indomitable spirit, asserting pride, identity as a community or a sub-culture and incorporating the need, no the right, to express oneself – an understanding that could have led to acceptance and joyful participation from the beginning.

The dilemma the early organizers of the yearly Carnival faced was that it depended solely on funding from agencies like the Arts Council, the Royal Borough of Kensington, the Greater London Arts Association (G.L.A.A.) and the Commission for Racial Equality (C.R.E.), some of whom sought to impose conditions on how it should be organised and routed, whereas the very nature of 'mas', as it is known, is that such controls should be minimal.

Today the commercial exploitation of Carnival without respect for the true spirit of mas has further undermined the whole process. The vast corporate sponsorship of the event has defused what was an act of defiance and the right to march, into mere exoticism. Big business sponsoring multiculturalism is a travesty of what it should be. Multiculturalism is not about exoticism and skin-deep integration but an intertwining of, and respect for, all cultural groups within society. It is perhaps ironic that the Notting Hill Carnival has recently received its highest accolade, leading the way at the official Royal procession during the Queen's Golden Jubilee Celebrations. As a reporter in *The Guardian* newspaper commented:

> Notting Hill Carnival's journey from a response to race attacks in 1958 to pride of place on the Mall in 2002, passing revelry, riot and resistance on route, is both powerful and painful. It is the tale of how a marginalized community built, protected and promoted what is now the largest street party in western Europe, using the radical cultural politics of the Caribbean to confront Britain's racist political culture. [Gary Younge]

Once a ritual where black people sought to celebrate their identity and creativity and where anyone could join in, playing mas is now mere spectacle rather than creative liberation, providing the uninhibited street party ambiance – steelpan music, pulsing sound systems, elaborate costumes – a jamboree for all and sundry. But this is not a true expression of cultural diversity. As the Guyanese writer Wilson Harris has observed:

> the greatest danger of cultural hubris is that it can conceal the latent seeds of fascism that lie hidden in so many societies in the late 20th Century....In this light the complex ramifications of carnival possess a practical bearing on the politics of our age and on what we tend to call 'human rights' or the values of freedom".[from *Carnival*]

A former head of the C.R.E., Sir Herman Ousley, pointed out in a recent article in *The Guardian*, that the word *multiculturalism* has been hijacked to serve the agendas of the scare-mongering racist media. This was indeed a strong indictment of the situation in which we find ourselves. Nevertheless, I believe that this issue must be discussed within the framework of the existing paradigm here in the West – the endemic racism that is a de facto element in the equation involving native and immigrant.

The present incumbent at the C.R.E.[1], Trevor Phillips, rightly considers that multiculturalism is 'in danger of being a sleight of hand in which ethnic minorities are distracted by tokens of recognition, while being excluded from the real business. The smile of recognition has turned into a rictus grin on the face of institutional racism'. [*The Guardian* 28 May 2004]. For him the ideal would be one nation, many faces:

> Integration only works if it both recognises newcomers' differences and extends complete equality. Celebrating diversity but ignoring inequality inevitably leads to the nightmare of entrenched segregation... the equality of the ghetto is no equality at all.

In other words, multiculturalism should not be about integration per se but about cultural plurality – to learn and benefit from its diversity. It is not about separation but about respect and the deepening awareness of Unity in Diversity. What is required is an integrative capacity that can pave the way for a better understanding of the basic commonality that exists in all multiplicity, a wholeness within an implicate order of interconnectedness.

It is time to move on to confront the real dangers of racism, discrimination and fanaticism.   A secular culture based on

---

[1] The C.R.E. was wound up in September 2007, its duties subsumed by the Commission for Equality and Human Rights with Phillips at the helm.

consumerism, competition and opportunism creates a materialistic society. Eclectic and superficial, it appropriates and devalues even those things which in themselves have value. It devalues as 'fads' any oppositional cultural trends, as for instance those towards holism, ecology, natural healing and reconciliation, ascribing its own face-value image to them. The prevalent computer-designed, global T.V. culture imposes its own spiritual impoverishment on everything it encounters. 'Multiculturalism', which is essentially about cultural pluralism and respect for other cultures, is subsumed, trivialised and incorporated into the prevalent fashionable pseudo-culture. Even the arts have been trivialised, resulting in the loss of such a talent as the theatre director Peter Brook whose *Mahabharata* failed to find a home in London.

Conclusion

I'm afraid that I'll have to close on a paradoxical note. I have pleaded on behalf of Diversity, on behalf of the globalisation of spirit above matter; that any concept of multiculturalism worth its salt, can only be understood within a holographic, non-dual paradigm. But its implementation will not be easy. It would require a multi-disciplinary, multi-dimensional ethic, which may be impossible to achieve. Each culture will maintain its own intrinsic value and at the same time would be expected to contribute to the benefit of the whole society in some way (an extrinsic value). But this does not mean that all cultures can contribute equally to the overall well being of a predominantly secular state.

Today, we may agree theoretically (politically correctly?) that we all have the same intrinsic rights to certain freedoms but that does not mean to say that we are all equal in all respects. Some of us are better musicians, for instance; or thinkers or whatever. Some of us may aspire to creating a more caring, spiritual dimension into our lives, something that the dominant culture has rejected. My point is that qualitative differences that may contribute to the good of the whole society may be rejected out of hand by the host culture as irrelevant, a clash between different perceptions of reality.

It would appear that the concept of an ideal multicultural society would be almost impossible to achieve, for how can one expect a predominantly secular society to understand this wider holistic concept which includes the rights of all the individuals who make up the society, and at the same time take on the responsibilities that those rights demand, for instance, in the case of a culture with an inward looking, separatist religion (a culture with a fundamental qualitative difference). For although it has an intrinsic value, and so intrinsic rights, nevertheless, it may not be contributing to the overall benefit of the society.

A case in point is the Muslim concept of personal law; how can this be accommodated within the overall common law of the present legal system? It is, as I've already said, a matter not of integration or of accommodation but one of negotiation. But first we need to develop a global perspective – to move from hybridity to heterosis; to a tolerant inclusive ideology that does not preclude a spiritual understanding of the universe – that everything is connected, that balance can resolve what has been seen as the clash of civilizations and the apparent duality of all existence, so leading to unity in diversity.

What is needed is a revaluation of how we interpret our diverse multicultural world. Multiculturalism, properly interpreted, can provide a model that can accommodate diversity of all kinds – cultural, philosophical and religious, so that we can create a world without conflict and strife. Britain, because of the lessons of Empire, is ideally placed to assume this role of accommodation and concern for all peoples, for our planet and indeed for our survival.

3: Black History, once a year: cure or concession?

A version of this essay was first published online by ITZCaribbean.com during Black History Month 2009.

Black History Month organizers often ask me to give presentations in October on the basis that an annual coming together may give a sense of belonging to the 'Black' community. Other representatives of that community are more sceptical, likening this one-a-year dosage to a limited concession at best. At worst, they see it as mere appeasement – a sop to encourage deprived communities to conform to the status quo.

I have come to question more and more the true motives behind this annual sequence of events. Whenever I have appeared at a venue in those communities I have been aware of a kind of euphoria reflecting the great need of our people, that they feel at last they are being recognized and accepted as equal citizens; and in a sense it would be churlish to deprive them of this sense of 'belonging'.

Appearing in a mostly 'white' venue is just the opposite. One is always aware of the possibility that such occasions can be officially approved rituals, mere concessions to alleviate the sense of deprivation suffered for the other eleven months of the year, but is nonetheless prepared to 'give it a go.' Regrettably, my experience has mostly realised this fear – of events roughly put together at the last moment, poorly publicised and tainted by poor organization and programming. Attendances are often small, audiences being made up largely of black people travelling from their own communities to catch some of the action, only to find none.

On the ground then, my own circumstances have led me to conclude that BHM is more concession than cure for society's failure to come together. It is difficult to take issue with those in the

'Appeasement' camp who see it as more crumbs off the white man's table and a field day for Black Race Relations predators. Having said that, I wanted to look again at the history of 'Black History' and see what positive vibrations might be encouraged.

I strived for concord,
unity in diversity:
effort still unheard.

now the climate's changed
awash with funds
of appeasement
floods that feed
the seasonal scramble;
tropical islanders
grabbing trade of
temperate tourists –
crumbs off history's imperial table

Shame
a clutch of activists
will bite the bait –
you can have de money
if you don't buck the State;
access via minimal concession

pawns in achromatic
game
that loads
the dice
of light and dark
of men and mice.

predators
oblivious to their second
class status,
acquiesce,
ignore the historical

perspective
how they were dat
now dis
empowered.

A version of this poem appears in *Rivers of Time*

A Brief History

What is not generally known in England is that Black History Month originated in America in 1926 as Negro History Week. The month of February was selected in deference to Frederick Douglass – the great Black American abolitionist, statesman and reformer of the 19th century – and Abraham Lincoln who were both born in that month.

Black History Month was adopted in London in October 1987 as part of African Jubilee year. The decision to make this an annual event each October was endorsed by the Association of London Authorities. From its early beginnings in African America, a commemoration of 'Negro' history has been expanded into one of 'Black' history. But what does the word 'Black' really mean today? Not so long ago it denoted a collection of communities of various origins who came to be known as 'Black' following increased immigration after the war, their only similarity being that they were not white. 'Blackness' was later adopted as a useful political stance – a point of resistance – in the face of overt racism and oppression in the late 1960s and early 70s and since then the contributions made to Britain by migrant communities have been many. These days 'Black' has been divorced from 'Asian' as a term, so in the context of this paper I am referring to people of African descent – many from the Caribbean – who are now British.

From *Week* we have moved to *Month*. But today any calendar month of the year would be appropriate for celebrating Black history. Throughout our recent history there have been many Black heroes – from Equiano and Toussaint L'Ouverture to W.E.B.

DuBois, Cheikh Anta Diop, George Padmore, Marcus Garvey, Martin Luther King, Nelson Mandela, Kwame Nkrumah, Jomo Kenyatta, Frantz Fanon, Aimé Césaire, Euzhan Palcy [film maker], Malcolm X, Mary Seacole, Rosa Parks and Claudia Jones to name but a few. There is a seemingly unending list of revolutionaries, world leaders, activists, scientists[1], writers such as Chinua Achebe and Ngugi Wa Thiongo, and scholars like J.J. Thomas, Adu Boahen, J.C.de Graft Johnson and Ivan Van Sertima. We have witnessed the far-reaching impact of black music in the jazz of Duke Ellington, Charles Mingus, Charlie Parker, Miles Davis, John Coltrane, Quincey Jones and Herbie Hancock. More and more we are made aware of important professionals and workers on world culture, of entertainers and sportsmen of the calibre of Mohamed Ali, Viv Richards, Brian Lara, Pele, and Tiger Woods.

Black history month, it seems to me, has come to reflect only the second-class status of black people within British society. A mere distraction or act of appeasement, it minimises black history and achievements, ignoring the true historical perspective of the contribution of black people. White children as well as black [who still experience racism] should learn that all our histories are inextricably linked, so changing the way they perceive themselves and the world. Black history in Britain dates back to the presence of African troops in the Roman armies. There was also a significant black presence in England even before the days of European conquest of Africa, the Americas and the Caribbean, and slavery and the heinous crimes perpetuated by Europeans. Black history also dates back to the civil rights movement of the 1960s and the ongoing struggle against racial discrimination. This reality can only be transmuted by unearthing the darkness of the human psyche in the context of colour: being Black and trapped in a White culture;

---

[1] See *Blacks in Science: Ancient and Modern* ed. Ivan Van Sertima. New Brunswick: Transaction, 1983.

being White and caught in an ambush of denial – the chequered history from which we must all learn – black or white[2].

For black people this would mean rediscovering the knowledge of who they really are, thus making themselves able to contribute positively to the healing of society. Their mere presence here is already making Europe confront its racism.

As early as 1959, the Trinidadian activist Claudia Jones, editor of the pioneering *West Indian Gazette* organised the first Notting Hill Carnival as a positive response to the so-called race riots there. Her belief was that the spirit of Carnival might displace racial tension. My West Indian hero was always Aimé Césaire, the still under-rated Martiniquan teacher, poet and philosopher who died only recently. His great work, *The Cahier*, was a call for a return to our native human values, to recognise that Nature is alive and bounteous and that we should not abuse her. Frantz Fanon, author of *The Wretched of the Earth* – the bible of the Black Power movement in 1960s America – was perhaps Césaire's best-known pupil. The Black Power movement knew about 'Black is Beautiful' but alas only on a superficial level, failing to recognise the dream of returning to natural values. Césaire wrote in his poem, 'you know it is not by hatred of other races that I prosecute for mine... All that I would wish is to answer the universal hunger... to prescribe this unique race free to produce... the succulence of fruit. Look. The tree of our hands is for all.'

In *The Way of the West* I said that the black man having reclaimed his authentic history and recovered his lost soul, must not fall into the trap of aspiring to assimilate into the so-called civilized values of his former oppressors. On the contrary, he must search out a different way. One obvious route would be to revert to the traditional values of community and caring; celebrating the intrinsic goodness of ancient African life and rites of passage; the 'being'

---

[2] See my book *Blackness and the Dreaming Soul*. Edinburgh: Shoving Leopard, 2007.

mode as opposed to the 'having' of Western culture, encapsulated in the Tswana concept of Modimo, where all life is sacred.

Surely it is time to challenge the Eurocentric nature of historiography, which still ignores its debt to the great civilisations of the world – India, China, Sumeria, Mesopotamia and Egypt. Egypt is of course an African country and all our knowledge of mathematics and philosophy originated in Africa where Pythagoras, the father of Greek civilization, (from which we trace our cultural and philosophical heritage knowledge) studied in the temples for twenty-one years. I have suggested elsewhere that Black people themselves have forgotten their birthright; that Africa was also the birthplace of the human race [the Mitochondrial Eve] where modern human history began. People of the African diaspora suffered tremendously from colonisation of the mind. They are still unable to disentangle themselves from the identity of 'collective victim', rooted in the experience of colonialism and the memory bank of slavery, which falsely gives them a sense of solidarity – a position that engenders further rejection, one which I call the 'black trap' in *The Way of the West*. In order to challenge the status quo, a clear understanding of the mechanics of this process is needed.

The Way Forward

Pride in one's blackness is just a part of a negative definition of self and needing to state that one is black and proud would be like trying to defend the obvious. This kind of pride is the other side of the coin of colonialism, the hubris of white institutions being the other.

The Association of London Authorities endorsed BHM in Britain in 1987, the very same year that saw the last Concord Multicultural Festival in Britain – a countywide event in Gloucestershire of which I was Director. The year before there had been a similar countywide Concord Festival in Devon. The previous three years had seen weekend Concord festivals in seventeen of Britain's main inner cities. Concord was set up by me in early 1980 to celebrate the cultural diversity within Britain as a result of the race riots that were rife at the time. Its object was to include all racial minorities and not just the black community. At the time, however, the notion of 'Multiculturalism'[3] was resisted and our work though impressive, filling major theatres throughout the country, never received the support that it needed from the Arts Council, County Councils and media.

The inauguration of Black History Month was a very poor response to what I believe is necessary if we are to achieve a fair society for all. Concord was not just about Black cultural events but there to celebrate the wide cultural diversity within Britain.[4]   A report on Concord in Devon, was also published by the Gulbenkian Foundation in 1987 [ironically the very year BHM was adopted in London] and provides a workable blue print for the arts, not only for the arts of minorities. Was all this work in vain? Even today the Arts Council have not acknowledged what we achieved and could still do to foster good relations within society. They still are locked in the same pattern of condescension and separation. As far as I can see nothing much has changed in the last two decades – just lip service to multiculturalism.

What I would propose is that funds should be allocated all year round instead of for just one month in the calendar year for a proper acknowledgement of our one history – to teach the history of Empire, not just cultural events. I suggest that a more detailed exposition of activities and learning should be promoted in a year-round approach to Black history, not just by local authorities but

---

[3] By 'multiculturalism', I don't mean the current idea of a number of separate groups held under one umbrella of tolerance but instead a true cross-cultural exchange.

[4] Chapter 5, "Concord" of *Blackness & the Dreaming Soul* gives a full account of those Festivals.

also in the media.

Spending could be at the discretion of local authorities and educational bodies. They could arrange well-structured events in conjunction with other bodies to ensure that there are no clashes of timetable so that a potential audience could witness them all rather than having to choose because of a concentration into a single month. Indeed, the greatest disadvantage of allocating just one month to all things black is that too many events are crowded into a short space of time. Also, some organisers of events will not care about the quality of events to be presented and so a lot of money is spent indiscriminately and planning and advertising can be slipshod.

A good example of what has been achieved by persistent lobbying over many years by the Equiano Society among others, is that now the story of Equiano[5] is being compulsorily taught at Key Stage 2 (aged 11-14) in all British schools [since September 2008] – not only during the month of October. But perhaps what is most urgently needed is in-service training for teachers, many of whom may still treat teaching about Equiano as a one-off exercise in exoticism. The whole issue of slavery in human history (which still exists in many forms) should also be explored, but not in our present climate of denial.

Before we decide upon a calendar of socially relevant events, we would do well to look again at who and what we are and begin to know like Césaire that the tree of our hands is for all.

---

[5] Olaudah Equiano (c.1745-97) was an African writer whose autobiography *The Interesting Narrative of Olaudah Equiano or Gustavus Vassa, the African* was published in 1787. A former slave who earned enough to buy his freedom, Equiano was a leading campigner for the abolition of the slave trade.

4. PAN AS COSMIC SYMBOL

This essay is based on an account of the evolution of the steel pan of Trinidad and Tobago, first presented in *Ring of Steel* and then revisited in *Blackness & the Dreaming Soul*.

The Birth of Pan

In the nineteenth century, the British attempted to control Carnival in Trinidad by banning the drum. This act was as cruel as destroying the language of the slaves had been. It led, however, to the evolution of the tambour bamboo bands in which bamboo 'reeds' were cut to varying lengths and music made by striking them on the ground or with sticks. During World War II, when Carnival itself was banned, the steel band evolved – appropriately from the tambour bamboo bands. At the end of the war, ingenious Trinidadians commandeered oil canisters left behind by the American forces and in a remarkably short period of time, transformed them into finely tuned melodic and harmonic instruments. These were to become a symbol of unity in the diversity so characteristic of the Caribbean territories as a whole.

The development of 'pan' as the instrument came to be called has paralleled the development of calypso and carnival in which the right to masquerade (what Trinidadians call 'play mas') is deeply rooted in the archetypal human and Dionysian need for a sense of meaning and validation. Dionysus, was not the god of drunkenness but the god of 'ecstatic vision' and we each need our ecstasy. If we do not get it legitimately, we will get it in an illegitimate way. Carnival, or Mas, is not only an ongoing re-enactment of historical reality but a psychic process, integrating the dark and the light, the masculine and the feminine, leading to individuation.

In 1995, I was asked by Macmillan to write a simple, large format picture book about the evolution of the steelpan of Trinidad and Tobago and from the very start of my research I realized that I was dealing with something very special and quite magical: the mythic story of the only acoustic instrument to be invented in the twentieth century. It was the story of the transmutation of industrial waste material into a musical instrument, which led me to explore the nature of sound and the harmonics of music.

In making steelpans the tops of the drums are sunk into a concave surface. This is followed by marking the notes and grooving, all of which disturb the molecular and crystalline balance of the steel which is corrected by tempering – the drums are heated for a specific time over intense heat to make the metal stronger and more ductile, the soul of the material lingering on, induced into liquid iridescent sound colours or overtones. The pioneers of this mythical process were unintentionally working as alchemists in that Alchemy involves a base metallic material, the outward form of which has to be first destroyed, the energy released and then reunited. Then heat is applied, blackening the substance, something known as nigredo. The goal of Alchemists was not just the materialist transmutation of base metal into gold but of a deeper understanding of the processes of transformation and creation. Much despised at first, the steelpan is now the national instrument of Trinidad. It has healed a divided society and it is played by all races. Today the music of pan resonates around the world, an image I sought to capture in *Ring of Steel* thus:

> The moon, a luminous disc
> hangs over the pan yard
> silent now
> the pandemonium long since ended...
> a lone pan man stayed on, musing...
> hung over his silver disk
> communing with the one above
> cascading arpeggios of moonlight
> improvising a silvery thread of melody

According to a recent computer generated hypothesis, the primordial matter of the Universe arranges itself, because of gravity, in thin filaments, which the cosmologists describe as a Cosmic Spider's web. It is a strange coincidence that one of the earliest versions of the steelpan which spawned the modern 'tenor pan', was known as a 'spider web pan', with notes tuned in a cycle of fourths and fifths. The primordial matter of the Universe is thus none other than the prima materia of the Alchemists from which all things evolve.

In *Ring of Steel*, I proposed that the universal appeal of steelpan music might be due to its special harmonic structure, although I made it clear that research still had to be done into the acoustics of the instrument. I also suggested that steelpan music produces healing natural harmonics – unstruck vibrations by virtue of its unusual and complex acoustics and tuning (the harmonics or partials are tuned in).[i] What seemed certain is that the sound the instrument makes follows the rules of Physics, which are universal. The overtone series is pure sound and not the product of Western tempered tuning. It may well be that steelpan music bridges both and that an exploration into the world of pan will not only be about steel drums, but also about the true meaning and significance of the word 'pan' ('all' in Greek) – it has certainly led me to an understanding that everything in creation has a harmonic base and that metaphysics is part of reality.

I no longer agree as I did in that book, with Joachim-Ernst Berendt's statement that the 'ears' of the world experience the teleological nature of the Western system of harmony, that is that all cultures contain the 'germ cells' of western music. Although I do stand by the main tenet of the book – that the creation of the steelpan was an alchemical process – I did not at the time quite understand how I myself was being transformed by studying the underlying principles of the harmonics of music.

It took more than a decade for this transformation to work but it gradually dawned on me that Western culture had come adrift. The difficulty in understanding 'pan' – as symbol – seemed to arise out of a rift with 'the East' and with Africa, home of the Mitochondrial Eve. I wrote my next book, *Blackness & the Dreaming Soul* to tease out what I saw as unifying forces in divided times. At the time, I was particularly taken by the realisation that the western world had hived 'science' away from 'soul' thus losing the alchemy that I had begun to understand in my investigation into 'pan'. It seemed to me that as things stood, scientists would demand empirical proof in all fields of enquiry. But the fact is that scientific method is not suitable to all fields of study. Empirical proof is as one sided as is, say, reductionism. Scientific method involves formulating a hypothesis and testing it empirically, i.e. if it cannot be measured by external instruments, it is not a fit subject for Science. What the empiricists did not take into account was the fact that the human body itself is a measuring device of remarkable complexity. According to the *Oxford Reference Dictionary*, empirical proof relies on observation and experiment, and not on theory but at the same time defines empiricism as the theory that regards sense experiences as the only source of knowledge. How, we may well ask, can scientific proof be based on an empiricism which is only a theory?

The Pythagorean Comma

One way I believe we can address the dilemma brought about by a reliance on a so-called empirical knowledge, is by considering music and our 'empirical' sense-experience of hearing in regard to the phenomenon known as the Pythagorean comma. In understanding the implications of the comma, I have been able to come full circle to, or should I say, to the next rung of the evolutionary spiral of, the latest scientific paradigm – string theory, the possibility of a unified theory of everything! This essay seeks to explain the notion of the comma and to make the case once more for pan as cosmic symbol.

The study of harmonics can be traced back to Pythagoras, the sixth century BC Greek philosopher and if pursued, will take us to that mysterious comma which was named after him. His theory of the harmony of the spheres was itself most likely derived from the Egyptian sidereal musical scale. He studied for twenty-one years in Egypt and the school which he later set up in Crotone, Southern Italy, was based on Egyptian mathematical and religious (*pan* theistic) principles.

In his book on the life of Pythagoras, the historian Iamblichus, describes how the Greek philosopher, was walking past a brazier's shop, when he heard 'hammers beating out a piece of iron'. The hammers were producing sounds that 'accorded' with each other. Going into the shop he found that those that sounded well together had weights that were related – twice, three times or half the weight of one another. He applied what he had discovered to various instruments, to pipes, reeds, monochords, triangles and to instruments known as patellae or pans. He had in fact discovered the overtone series. The sounds he heard – 'hammers beating out a piece of iron' – have resonated down the centuries: some Trinidadians still refer to playing pan as beating iron!

In the overtone scale, also known as the harmonic series, the notes rise in exact numerical relationships to the fundamental. Taking the fundamental as the first note, the second note is twice its frequency (an octave); the third note is three times the fundamental (a fifth in musical terms); the fourth, four times the frequency (the next octave) and so on. As we move further away from the fundamental, the intervals between the octaves become progressively smaller (i.e. the ratios between the numbers become smaller and smaller the greater their number).

Overtones are in pure mathematical proportions, or whole number ratios, and the most consonant of these are the octave (2/1) and the fifth (3/2). But no matter how many times you put a fifth on top of a fifth you will never reach an exact octave. A succession of twelve musical fifths is almost the same as seven octaves, but not exactly. Starting, for instance, from a fundamental C, a series of twelve perfect fifths will arrive at B#, which is slightly higher in pitch to that of the original C. This discrepancy in pitch is known as the Pythagorean comma, because Pythagoras was thought to be the first to discover it. A comma is the interval between two almost identical notes. To bridge this discrepancy, Western music, since the Seventeenth century, has adopted what is called equal temperament in which commas do not exist; the interval between each of the twelve semitones of the octave is exactly equal. Apart from the octave, all the notes are out of tune to the natural principles of resonance. The introduction of Equal Temperament has forced the natural spiral of perfect fifths into a circle of imperfect fifths by the process of flattening them 1/12 of a Pythagorean comma, thus equalizing the B# and C. It has eliminated the 'problem' posed by the Pythagorean comma and allows for chord changes and shifts in key.

Early western music was modal, each piece based on a single scale or mode and not on chords which are constantly changing. Modal music, like plainsong and Gregorian chant, has for me a spiritual, feel-good quality. Its intervals have a universal consonance. Despite the obvious advantages, Western music has moved away from natural harmonic resonances and has threatened the music of other cultures. Accepting the comma would be to admit the limitations of the human intellect, that empirical proof is only an illusion of science. Perhaps the symbolic value of the Pythagorean comma is that infinite and intangible side to our world that we cannot explain. E.T. is indeed an alien in that it does not accord with the laws of physics. If physical laws can be ignored there can be no such thing as empirical proof. At the very time empiricism first was introduced in Enlightenment Europe, clocks were becoming commonplace and the first Astronomer Royal, John Flamsteed, [1646-1720] claimed that "The clocks have proved rational conjecture to be a very truth". Clock faces are divided in twelve equal hours just as the circle of musical fifths has replaced the natural spiral of the Pythagorean comma. In 1752 the Gregorian calendar was adopted in Britain, this being another symptom of our disconnection from the natural, 'organic' sense of time, that is lunar time.

The switch to equal temperament at the end of the eighteenth century began in earnest with the Industrial Revolution and the standardization of pianos and organs. Today, the *New Oxford Companion to Music* (1983) actually defines Just Intonation, a system of tuning instruments derived from the natural Harmonic Series[1], as a system of tuning in which the notes furthest from the fundamental 'are severely out of tune, hence the introduction of Equal Temperament as a substitute for the "natural" non-tempered scale'. One can safely speculate that Equal Temperament is part of the foundation of modern Western civilization, based on technology and has contributed to our separation from nature and to the ultimate triumph of science – rationality now supersedes reality... And so we have lost that sense of magic the ancient Greeks once embraced. Considered to be irrational, the Pythagorean comma is of no import, because we need to be in control, not only in the sacred realm of music, but of time itself.

When equal temperament was first implemented it was generally considered inharmonious, producing 'a harmony extremely coarse and disagreeable' (Robert Smith 1759). The father of scientific acoustics, Hermann von Helmholtz (1821-1894), who had proposed the first scientific theory of consonance and dissonance, claimed that equal temperament 'had a deplorable effect on music practice.' Since its introduction, much of the early music by the great composers is no longer heard as it was written

---

[1] 'Just Intonation is limited to one key. Its aim is to make the intervals as concordant as possible with both one another and with the harmonics of the key note and of closely related notes. Most of the frequency ratios can be expressed in terns of comparatively small numbers, indicating consonant harmonies' – from *Science & Music* by Sir James Jeans.

e.g. J.S. Bach's vocal and organ music and Handel's works for clavichord and harpsichord which were written in the mean-tone system[2]. All this was to change when, in 1723, Bach himself adopted the system. His *Wohl-temperiertes Klavier* (Well Tempered Clavier) covers all twenty four major and minor keys and 'enabled compositions in all keys to be played without disagreeable discords'. [Sir James Jeans: *Science & Music*] It also facilitated modulation and transposition. Resisted at first, equal temperament gradually caught on and spread dramatically, swamping the music of all other cultures.

It should be noted that the tempered scale was in fact proposed as early as 1492 by the Spanish musician, Bartolo Rames, and by 1636, the French mathematician Marin Mersenne was aware of it. [Jeans]. It was also known to Chu Tsai-Yu, a Chinese Prince, over a hundred years before Bach adopted it. The Chinese, however, have stayed with the natural intervals as sacrosanct to the relationship between man and the Cosmos.

In the West, we learned to hear the inexact intervals of equal temperament as true. I was brought up in a musical family. My mother taught the piano and I myself could play *Für Elise* by Beethoven, and some of the relatively easy pieces for students of the piano. My ears were trained to equal temperament as my mind had been to Western versions of history and, more importantly, to the dualism that underpins the Western paradigm, a subject explored in more detail in *Blackness and the Dreaming Soul*. In tempering the musical intervals we have tampered with nature, claiming the product as the real thing – reality. Perhaps that is why the world is in the state that it is in today.

Herman Hesse in his book *Musique*, seems to be saying the same thing: 'The music of a harmonious epoch will be calm and serene and the government will be moderate. The music of an

---

[2] Mean-tone scale is an earlier attempt to solve the 'problem' caused by the Pythagorean comma.

agitated epoch will be shouting and loud and the government will be wrong. The music of a State on the decline is sentimental and sad and the government will be in danger'[3]. This corresponds with the view of the ethno-musicologist, Alain Danielou, who believed that for the world to be in a state of equilibrium, its different elements would need to be harmonized. Music expressed the relations between human and cosmic order and must respect the exact intervals on which these relations are based. 'Disregard for such an obvious law necessarily leads to a breakdown of equilibrium and social disorder...by allowing such aberrations as equal temperament, the lack of a proper theoretical foundation will in all probability drive the European classical system to complete decadence'.[4]

For many years now, I have been a keen student of the ancient Chinese wisdom known as the Tao Te Ching and if it has taught me anything, it is that life is paradoxical and true knowledge or wisdom elusive; that there is no consonance without dissonance. The tempered scale and the natural scale are all contained within the holographic whole. Commas are part of the harmonic fabric of natural resonance. As we have seen, a series of Pythagorean fifths creates an infinite spiral not a closed circle. The Pythagorean Comma (expressed in numerical terms, 1.0136) was none other than the tiny gap or sacred number of the gods of the ancient Egyptians which applied not only to music but to astrology and cosmology. The Well Tempered Clavier is wonderful music; my ears do not hear the slight dissonances. Indeed, the noted British scientist, Sir James Jeans has stated that 'The indisputable dissonances of equal temperament no longer distress us in the way that they seem to have distressed our more fastidious predecessors.' [*Science & Music*] Nonetheless, because of the importance that I attach to the 'comma',

---

[3] Cited in Fabien Mamam: *The Role of Music in the Twenty-First Century*
[4] from *Music & The Power of Sound*

I should like to set out some of the ways the natural scale has been employed over the years, by cultures both western and eastern.

Tranquility and Healing

Pan music accentuates the fifth interval, the most consonant interval, used throughout the ages to invoke the divine. I speculated in *Ring of Steel* that the steelpan produces healing natural harmonics, an infinite spiral of fifths beyond the circle of fifths[5] which is the basis of equal temperament.

The universal consonance and appeal of early music have been known to have a healing effect. This was demonstrated by Dr. Alfred Tomatis, a French physician and researcher in the field of audio-psycho-phonology (a science of re-educating the ear) when he demonstrated that the reason monks in a monastery in France were becoming lethargic and falling ill, was because their normal routine of chanting had been suspended for some months. When the practice was re-instituted they became well again. Tomatis believed that sacred chant, rich in high frequency harmonics has a neuro-physiological, transformative and healing effect on mind and body. The Tomatis method employs an Electronic Ear especially developed by the physician over very many years of research, in which sounds – particular kinds of music— are filtered to emphasize the harmonics. By hearing these higher frequencies, Tomatis claimed that the ear could be re-educated and many conditions, like autism and schizophrenia, inter alia, cured.

Through a study of Sacred Geometry I first became aware of the relationship between sound and form, that a harmonic structure underlies all creation, not only in the fields of mathematics, geometry, architecture, philosophy, physics and many other natural

---

[5] The circle of fifths is no more than a graphic representation of keynotes with their signatures in the shape of a circle; the notes progress clockwise in ascending fifths: C_G_D etc.

sciences (as they relate to our body structures and sense organs) but also to sound and music therapy. The deep structure of music is the same as the deep structure of everything else. The musicologist, Rudolph Haas, discovered that harmonic proportions exist in chemistry – molecules strive for symmetry. The irrational Pythagorean comma may be beyond the grasp of whole numbers as is the Fibonacci series in the spiral growth patterns we see in nature. The irrational numbers, the intangibles, are the Mystery which cannot be grasped by Science alone.

> Beyond form, it cannot be seen
> beyond sound, it cannot be heard
> intangible, it is not to be grasped
> indefinable, these three merge into one
>   Tao Te Ching

Instead of seeing things in irrational numerical terms, we must somehow grasp them without being able to describe them in words.

> Shape clay into a vessel
> It is the space within that makes it useful

The space within, described in the Tao, is equivalent to the tiny gap or sacred number of the ancient Egyptian gods, referred to above. Remarkable as it may seem, it has been demonstrated that perception and awareness depend on a myriad of neuronal interactions within the brain. All nerve impulses have to jump a tiny gap (a synapse) between the axons and dendrites. How we interpret what we see may depend on how we perceive them.

Sir Isaac Newton discovered the full colour spectrum of light by viewing the light of the sun through a narrow slit between curtains, filtering it through a prism. The rays of the colour spectrum are to light what the harmonic series is to sound. Overtones are always present although not always filtered out by our hearing. But the rainbow of sound, the overtone series, can be heard, for instance, in the magical art of overtone singing. This kind of singing was first introduced to the West through the recent interest in world religious practices and music, for instance in the chanting of Tibetan monks and the many toned singing (known as throat singing) of the Tuvan people from Mongolia. It has led to a revival of interest into the nature of sound.

The great Sufi master, Hazrat Inayat Khan, has said that what we simply refer to as music 'is only a miniature from the music or harmony of the whole universe which is working behind everything, and which is the source and origin of nature. It is because of this that the wise of all ages have considered music to be a sacred art. For in music the seer can see the picture of the whole universe...' For him 'The cosmic system [works] by the law of music, the law of harmony; and whenever that harmony in the cosmic system is lacking in any way, then in proportion disaster comes to the world, and its influence is seen in the many destructive forces which are manifest there'.

The ancient Greeks were also deeply aware of this cosmic relationship of music to science and culture. They knew that the mathematical laws of music were the same as the laws that regulated harmony in all matters, from the growth patterns of plants to geometry and good government.

This magical connection between sound and all aspects of manifestation, including form, was integral to many cultures and a way of restoring harmony at all levels of society. Various modes of sound have been used down the ages for calming, stimulating and creating desired moods and it is said that these modes resonate with the endocrine system of the body. Music was integral to every aspect of ancient Chinese culture and government. According to the Yue ji, 'under the effect of music, the five social duties are without admixture, the eyes and the ears are clear, the blood and the vital spirits are balanced, habits are reformed, customs are improved, the empire is in complete peace'. [quoted by Danielou]

Indian classical music, with a history of three millennia, is modal, finding its true expression in improvisation, tone colour, embellishments and non-western intervals. As in jazz, improvisation is at its heart, connecting the musician to the subtle bodies or auras (the higher harmonics of the physical body) by activating the psychic centres, or *chakras*. For those of us who enjoy jazz, its characteristic 'blue' notes communicate in a similar way.

This was to a lesser extent true of the music of Arabia, Persia (Iran), Turkey, Japan, Tibet and Africa. African Music was said to be 'divine expression... medicine. Its intensity, its pitch, its timbre all translate the power of the gods into action among human beings and the physical world. Thus music can charm a person, send her/him into an altered state of consciousness: it can heal someone...' [Dr. A. E. Mereni in *The British Journal of Music Therapy Vol.10 No.1*]

The notion of the potential healing power of sound has remained with me ever since I started my investigations into pan and its inextricable link with the strange creature known as the Pythagorean comma. When I first experienced the way the 'soul' of the steel lingers on after heat treatment, into 'sound colour', I had no idea that these were overtones and a real life example of the Comma in action.

In Trinidad, in the middle of the twentieth century, the magical transmutation of industrial waste material – discarded oil drums – into a highly tuned percussion instrument took place in what I have termed an unintentionally alchemical way, that is, allowing for a deeper understanding of the processes of transformation and creation. I described in *Ring of Steel* how the instrument which emanated from the poorer districts of the island was despised by the colony's upper echelon; it is now the national instrument of Trinidad. It has healed a divided society and all races play it and today the music of pan resonates around the world. Even the Swiss have embraced and developed it!

What we need is a quantum leap in consciousness if we are to transcend the limitations of the prevailing paradigm that the West seeks to impose on the rest of the world. According to Itzhak Bentov; 'Knowledge moves in an ever-expanding upward spiral, which allows us to see from the higher turns of the spiral our previous knowledge in a broader perspective. Thus, Newton's mechanics have become a "special case" within Einstein's theory of relativity' [*Stalking the Wild Pendulum*]; in the same way as Einstein's theory of relativity had become a 'special case' in an endless spiral of cosmological theories purporting to be the final grand unified theory of everything. Another special case that strikes a cosmic chord is String Theory – that the Universe is composed of myriad vibrating strings and not the elementary particles of a previous model - the world is truly sound as Berendt claimed [*The World is Sound: Nada Brahma*].

Just as the Pythagorean cycle of musical fifths reach upwards in an infinite spiral, so it seems does consciousness. Harmonic conscious emptiness, symbolised by zero and the infinite spiral of harmonic energy ratios (the octave and the natural fifth) transport the listener to a deep level of consciousness. In Taoist terms, the harmonic ratios model the 'emptiness of the Absolute void circle'. Just as one cannot describe the Tao, the primordial, so one cannot describe the shift in consciousness which is beyond what we consider to be our bodies – even though we have been clued up about the synaptic gaps of our brains. Most of us identify with our bodies. They represent who or what we think we are. When we become able to go beyond that physical containment, beyond the tiny gaps in our minds, to find that vast space of which we are part, we become one with the ineffable Tao.

And the unique harmonic environment set up by the steel pan has the unexpected effect of taking us to this next level of consciousness. It is truly remarkable that a new musical instrument has affected so many people in a positive way in just half a century. Science will no doubt continue to probe the improbable but might it

be that the universal appeal of pan, that microcosmic sphere, is
because we are all entrained to the harmonic nature of the macro
cosmos? Pan, for me, is cosmic symbol; pan music, the music of the
spheres.

> Anansi the wise spider-man
> watched over us as we rode the inferno
> below the limbo depths
> of the middle passage.
> First he spun a thin thread
> straddling the Equator
> umbilical chord linking us to Africa;
> then wove a web of epic tales
> of trickery and survival
> tales of home, of ancestors
> of Ogun, god of war and iron;
> how one day his voice will resonate
> through his son.
> Pan.
> spiralling outwards,
> spanning the globe
> a ring of steel
> a healing web of sound.
> These things he foretold lest we forget:
> tales woven in his own image
> spherical spider web pan
> linking both hemispheres.
> Like a pebble
> dropped into the great void
> the sound of pan
> ripples outwards
> surfing the cosmic net

> from *Ring of Steel*.

END NOTE

---

[i] In Hindu musical theory there are two kinds of sound, ahata nada, struck sound, and anahata nada, unstruck sound. The former corresponds with our scientific understanding of sound vibration, the latter with what Pythagoreans called the music of the spheres. In Shabad Yoga, the Sound Current (also referred to as the Audible Life Stream) equates to the concept of limitless sound, the WORD, or Divine Creative power, or LOGOS. This yoga of the Divine Word utilizes Anahad Shabd or unstruck sound as an aid to spiritual development and liberation from the bonds of mind and matter while living here and now on earth. In the teachings of the Saints (Sant Nat), the soul (Surat) merges with the Word (Shabd) and is carried to the Source, the Godhead. It is a system of meditation that takes its followers to the highest attainable states of spiritual development and consciousness by developing the Audible Life Stream or Sound Current.

In Healing Sounds, Jonathan Goldman speculates that the fundamental may be the struck sound, whilst the harmonics which are created the unstruck. "Perhaps they are the bridge between the physical and the metaphysical". He quotes Pir Vilayat Khan "The overtones can be followed with the conscious mind and used as a 'Jacobs' ladder' to climb to other planes of consciousness": In other words, listening can be used as a tool for enhanced consciousness. "There is acknowledged an understanding of the Shabda, the 'Sound Current', which can be ridden like a flying horse to other planes of existence. This is accomplished through meditation on sound".

5. DECIPHERING HIDDEN CODES & SYNCHRONICITIES:

COINCIDENCE & MEANING

This essay is expanded from a description of the author's role in a 1960s sci-fi series, first published on the Cy Grant website.

The term 'synchronicity' emerges from the work of the Swiss psychologist Carl Jung. Synchronicities are simultaneous coincidences that seem to be meaningfully related; supposedly the result of the alignment of "universal forces" with the life experiences of an individual:

> a meaningful coincidence or correspondence of two or more outer and inner events which are causally unrelated occurring together in a supposedly meaningful manner; -a non-causal connection between two or more various phenomena (psychic and/or physical).

The 5th of November, 2009, saw the launch of Erica Myers-Davis' book *Under One Flag*, about the contribution of peoples from the Commonwealth who took part in WWII, a contribution which has not been officially recognized. Exactly one year previously, the 5th of November 2008, the very first black President of the USA was announced to the world – a black man in the White House. As if to confirm a synchronicity, the book's release had been put back from October – it had been intended for Black History Month – thus also defying the logic that Black History, or for that matter curriculum studies, should be relegated to one specific month of the year.

Our histories are inextricably intertwined, surely the point that *Under One Flag* is about. These events may not have been simultaneous but the change of climate has certainly demonstrated a marked change in attitudes. Aimed at the schools curriculum, the book is a very welcome and groundbreaking event, a synchronicity beyond simultaneous coincidence I feel.

There is, however, an issue that ought to be addressed at the very onset, in order to avoid misconceptions when reference is made to the colour or race of peoples from the Commonwealth, namely, the use of the word 'indigenous' in the subtitle to the book and in both Forewords, and of which school children should be made aware. 'Indigenous' means native or belonging naturally to a country. We are all indigenous, natives of the country of our birth, whether we are English or Eskimo.

Under One Flag is not a UFO, but a reality. There is a short profile of me making reference to my war memoir, *A Member of the RAF of Indeterminate Race.* My book is certainly not fiction but although it was published over three years ago, it has been ignored by the press. Now it seems, it will have a chance of seeing the light of day. The contribution of overseas servicemen has long been ignored. For me, personally, both publications are *meaningfully related.*

It happened that at the launch of the book, I was filmed chatting with the Duke of Edinburgh, me in a wheel chair (a 'centre of gravity' exchange?) who thought I was a war veteran of some Overseas Campaign. He seemed to be unaware that men from the Caribbean had flown as aircrew in the RAF.

Another example of this malaise can be demonstrated in the British film *Appointment in London*, 1954, in which a similar attitude prevailed. The story revolves around Bomber Command Squadron in 1943 and includes a brief reference to black aircrew, only lasting a few seconds, but which must have confounded the audience at the time. 'Wing Commander' Dirk Bogarde is seen to have a short word with a black airman. Given that one of the script writers was John Wooldridge, a commander of 105 Squadron RAF during WWII who would have been aware of the presence of black aircrew, it seems reasonable to assume that he inserted the scene into the movie as a mark of recognition and respect.

Under One Flag also documents the fact that I was instrumental in setting up with webmaster Hans Klootwijk, an online archive website of the 440 Caribbean air crew who flew with the RAF in WWII – and at the very time that President Obama was changing the consciousness of the Planet; yet another simultaneous occurrence!

The chain of events leading up to this is quite exceptional.

When in the early morning of Saturday, 26th June 1943, our Lancaster bomber, on its return leg after a successful raid over Gelsenkirchen in the Ruhr, was attacked by a German fighter over Holland and exploded in mid-air near the village of Nieuw-Vennep, south of Amsterdam, one of its engines fell through a farmhouse in the village killing the wife of the farmer.

The crash made such an impact on the young Joost Klootwijk – Hans' father – that he resolved, many years later, to reconstruct the events of that tragic night. He succeeded brilliantly in his ambition, having contacted the Air Ministry and other official bodies in Britain, Holland and Germany and over 20 eyewitnesses. With great perseverance, he recorded and documented the entire mission on the night of 25th/26th June 1943, when 473 bombers of the RAF Bomber Command took part, including 24 Lancasters from my own 103 Squadron. On that mission alone, the RAF sustained a loss of 34 aircraft over northern Holland, including thirteen Lancasters – two from my own Squadron.

Klootwijk was able to trace the airfield in England where my Lancaster Bomber had taken off, the name of the Squadron and even the total bomb load carried by that particular aircraft. He succeeded in tracing the members of the crew who survived, to learn their versions of events on that fateful night, the actual places where crew members had landed or died, and managed to obtain the testimony of villagers who witnessed the explosion and the immediate aftermath, including the role of the Germans and the Dutch policeman whose duty it was to hand over shot down air crew like myself and my mid-upper gunner, Geoffrey Wallis.

What is so extraordinary is that this constitutes a unique and complete record of the fate of just one of over 6.500 airplanes, mostly RAF, that came down in Dutch territory, on sea or land. Of these, an estimated 2,000 wreckages are still buried in the ground. About 450 crew are still listed as missing in action. Did the fact that a black airman was involved influence Kootwijk to write about the crash or was it just another example of meaningful connections beyond synchronicities?

One of the most striking aspects of this episode is that it touched so many lives – that in the midst of the horrors of war, we find the making and resolution of a personal tragedy in Holland, the formation of a lasting bond between Canadian (the pilot and tail gunner were Canadian), English, West Indian and Dutch, forged in the skies over The Netherlands and Germany, and a moving and compelling comment on both the bravery and brutality of war and its relevance to how we record our histories and make our realities.

Under One Flag also drew attention to the fact that I was responsible for setting up Concord Multicultural Festivals in the 1980s, celebrating the cultural diversity of Britain; an event obviously not lost on Corporal Johnson Beharry, VC when on the day of the book launch he thanked me for what I was doing 'for us'.

More significantly, the book notes that I voiced the puppet character Lieutenant Green in Gerry Anderson's sci-fi series, *Captain Scarlet & the Mysterons!* This is all good schoolboy stuff but is also an allegorical tale of the forces of good over evil at a time when our world was under threat of nuclear warfare. School children have followed the series over three decades now and have been impressed when they discovered my role as Lt. Green.

Synchronistic or not, there are some extraordinary meaningful coincidences involved regarding my appearances on TV. I believe that my regular appearances on the BBC *Tonight* programme singing the news in calypso, in the late 1950s may have influenced Anderson when he decided to cast me, a very visible black actor at the time. He could not have possibly known about my service record; that I had in real life been a Navigator of Lancaster bomber in WWII, giving flight directions to my pilot. Now I was to be cast in a similar role in a sci-fi TV series! Why me?

I was to learn that Anderson had also served in the RAF, albeit as part of National Service after the War, passing out at the rank of Leading Aircraftsman. His brother, Lionel, had been lost in the War over Holland, where I was shot down, flying one of the many Mosquitos which acted as homing beacons for British bombers and decoys for enemy radar systems.

Anderson's whole concept seemed to have religious connotations, the forces of good against evil: Colonel White (the Supreme Being) and Captain Scarlet (his son?) who is killed each time, but miraculously survives death because he is a Mysteron creation and therefore not actually mortal, whilst Captain Black is the Devil incarnate.

Was it just coincidence that the actor who voiced Captain Black was a white South African at the time of Apartheid and Ian Smith's Rhodesia? That actor, Donald Gray, a charming man no doubt, had a sticker on his car with the words 'Support Rhodesia' which I recall I queried at the time, much to his chagrin.

Was it also pure coincidence that both my surname and that of the puppet character I voiced began with the letters 'GR' – GRANT/ GREEN, or that the actor who voiced Captain Scarlet mimicked the voice of Cary Grant?

The BBC programme *Tonight* began with me, a black actor, singing the daily news in calypso. This was also the time (1957) that the calypso craze began world wide. That same year Harry Belafonte released his record breaking LP *Calypso*. Of course, these songs were not calypso but his world wide appeal was vast and immediate. The fact we looked so much alike caused a great deal of distress to both of us. I reacted by recording a mock calypso sending up the great man [*Bela-Calypso*].

The effect that both series had on black people watching TV in Britain was significant – for the very first time there was a positive image of someone they could relate to with pride.

Was it that the black presence in Britain could have a healing potential for society – that Britain was being forced to acknowledge its shadow, its past history of racism and slavery? Anderson broadcast his series initially between September 1967 and May 1968. April 1968 was the date that Enoch Powell made his 'Rivers of Blood' speech that brought the shadow into the open. Was the struggle between good and evil that the series seems to represent also prompting us to know each other and so reconstruct the way in which we make our reality?

The Civil Rights Movement in America had given impetus to the Women's Rights Movement. Captain Scarlet's Cloudbase was itself defended by female fighter pilots called Angels, one of whom, Melody, was black. Both *Captain Scarlet* and its American counterpart, *Star Trek*, came out about the same time [Star Trek dates from 1966-69], both series in which women as well as ethnic minorities were cast in meaningful roles. This was a powerful message for the young at the time and no doubt led to the changes in racial attitudes that are slowly healing our society. Both series captured the imagination of the younger generations thus creating a climate for a change of consciousness.

Again, the name SPECTRUM – the organisation with its Headquarters at Cloudbase – was a plausible representation of Heaven, where Colonel White, and his colour spectrum of Officers were based, protecting the world from the evil Mysterons on Mars (Hades). Captain Black (Satan) was an Archangel who had 'fallen from grace', a former Spectrum agent who was possessed by the Mysterons and who acted as their agent on earth. In the opening sequences he wears his black Spectrum uniform and is pictured standing outside a cemetery, thereby emphasising his connection with the dark forces. In two of my books, *Ring of Steel*, and *Blackness and the Dreaming Soul*, I compare the significance of the colour spectrum to that of the rainbow of sound, the laws of the physics of sound – the overtone series. The colour white incorporates all other colours as a single note in music, the fundamental, containing all the natural overtones or harmonics.

My colleague, Terrence Brathwaite, suggested to me that one could also see Lt. Green as a Western archetype of the African trickster god, Legba, messenger of and spokesman for the other Orishas. Legba is the keeper of the crossroads between the worlds, the messenger between human and divine worlds. He understands all languages (including that of the Mysterons), and acts as an interpreter for the Gods and opens the door to the spirit world. It is only through him that the other orishas (SPECTRUM agents of change) can be contacted.

I have suggested previously that the title, 'Only Connecting', of a Concord brochure seemed to imply that there is a guiding principle which operates beyond one's volition. I had run Concord Multicultural Festivals during the 1980s in all the major cities in Britain. This was one of a number of staging posts in my long career – starting with my life as an RAF officer, then an actor/singer, cultural activist, and a writer – which had unwittingly pointed to the fact that a new Consciousness is dawning, that we have to reconnect not only with the fact that there is a spiritual dimension to life but that this is essentially a holistic, non-dual reappraisal of the prevailing paradigm and our need to reconnect with our evolutionary journey out of Africa, our roots, our Mitochondrial Eve.

In this collection, I have advocated a reconnecting process via traditional African models, or through the ancient Chinese wisdom of the Tao, but we had seen way back in the 1980s, the importance for celebrating our Multicultural World – what I have called Unity in Diversity. Now I can see that the process of making this connection has been the main driving force of my life and still remains so. It's not about massaging one's ego I hope, but my life purpose! So do we remain unconscious or do we become the consciousness that will change our worldview? I believe that if we can consciously connect to 'Cosmic Consciousness' that that force will guide us. But maybe I should say that we are already connected but do not know it. And here's the paradox. Trying to connect can most likely preclude connecting (more ego, more wanting); while knowing that one is already connected requires no effort of mind. It is an allowing, an inner knowing, that allows the consciousness to guide, to transform not only the individual, but the collective unconsciousness of the prevailing paradigm and to integrate the Dark and the Light of the human soul.

As an analogy, we all use computers to connect us to the information that is out there provided by the wiz kids of Silicon Valley – all we need is a computer, a provider and a connection to our electricity supply – the information is all out there in the space around us. But we ourselves are super-computers. Just think about how our bodies and minds are connected, regulating all their systems without any effort on our part. We are all connected to the vast memory bank of Cosmic Intelligence. I call it Tao because it is primordial, containing All, the mother of all things. Some call it God – but for me that term implies separation – me, you, God, duality, confusion.

We are all part of the Tao; and with this knowledge we may learn just who and what we really are – creators of our own destiny and so awaken to the purpose of our lives! But first we will have to learn how to override the neurons in our brains – the synaptic gap between mind and 'no mind' – and so creating Unity in Diversity, finally become One with All.

6. Awake in the Dream

The original version of this piece was written in response to a call for essays by the SMN Review. It proved to be the spark for this collection and has been expanded to act both as summary and point of departure.

Every great dream begins with a dreamer... Always remember, you have within you the strength, the patience, and the passion to reach for the stars to change the world.
Harriet Tubman

Tell me what a man dreams and I'll tell you what he is
Arab proverb

The dreamer is consciousness itself... To awaken within the Dream is our purpose now. When we are awake within the dream a more benign and wondrous dream arise. This is the new earth.
Eckhart Tolle

When I first read the quoted passage from Tolle, I was immediately reminded of the dream of Chuang Tzu, the Taoist master, dreaming that he was a butterfly, dreaming it was Chuang Tzu and wondering who was the dreamer – himself or the caterpillar – wanting to know their true nature. These days I certainly feel like a fragile caterpillar in search of my true nature. It has been a long journey. I have rehearsed it again and again and the first five essays in this book bear witness to the often less than dream-like process. But having been reminded of the Taoist dream afresh I felt that I should explore the subject of dream a little further. Does the butterfly dream mean that the world is eternally in flux? Or is it that we *think* we have wakened from the dream but are still asleep? I know from meditating that the reawakening process is a special one. What if the butterfly is prompting us to make a new reality for ourselves by awakening to a new level of consciousness, a new outlook?

In writing this essay, I set out to expand upon the outline of my physical journey provided in *Beyond The Jargon* and to describe how my discovery of two life-changing books had altered its trajectory. And I do start off in this vein, until the butterfly flies in...

When I wrote my book *Blackness & the Dreaming Soul*, the title had seemed to come from somewhere I couldn't quite explain. But somehow the subtitle, *Race Identity and the Materialistic Paradigm*, came to my rescue. It was simply my frustration of having to live as an insider in a culture into which I was born and educated, yet at the same time without a sense of belonging– a de facto outsider. True, for a while I considered that I had at last joined the club, when as a young man I was commissioned as an Officer in the Royal Air Force[1] and flew as a navigator of a Lancaster bomber in World War II; also, having been shot down on a return mission over Germany, spending two years in a prisoner of war camp especially reserved for British Officers. Man, I did belong!

Later, I qualified as a Barrister at Law at the distinguished Middle Temple, not realising at the time that that great institution had strong connections with the slave trade that had underpinned the empire. Here was I, the great grandson of an African slave, colluding with my enslavers.

And though unaware of this link, any sense of belonging was soon shattered when I found that even if I were able to afford chambers, it would be some considerable time before I was able to earn a living. My applications for finding work as a lawyer met with a stony wall of silence. The stark reality about my status as a human being was being defined for me by the society and culture!

---

[1] The RAF changed its policy regarding the recruitment of colonial volunteers when things were not going so well in 1942

It has taken me years to understand that something was inherently wrong with this Western worldview – this paradigm of separation, division and endemic racism. It forced me to pursue a career in show business in which I was lucky to survive with a measure of success as an actor and singer – the first black face to be seen regularly on British television on the BBC's innovative and ground breaking *Tonight* programme of the late 1950s. But the seed had been planted – who was I and what?

My later life has been a journey of self-exploration, reading about the Civil Rights movement in America; Martin Luther King's dream for equality; Nelson Mandela's imprisonment for twenty-eight years on Robben Island for his dream for the rightful people of his country.

When Enoch Powell, the then Conservative MP for Wolverhampton made his inflammatory 'Rivers of Blood' speech, it signalled the inner city disquiet that rocked Britain in the late 1960s and early 1970s, with a loud echo in the early 1980s. I became a member of CARD [The Campaign Against Racial Discrimination] heading a long march to Downing Street whilst being jeered and booed along the way by striking Dockers. Was this the Britain I had fought for during the war? This incident forced me to take stock of my position within the racial frenzy that it stirred up, forcing me to take a stand. Could I ignore this and continue to live at peace with myself as a minor celebrity in a culture that rejected me?

I began writing poetry, producing a small collection, *Black Words*, which I toured around small venues, universities and fringe festivals. Some of these were printed in James Berry's *Bluefoot Traveller*, a pioneering anthology of West Indian British poetry.

Red
White blue
Brown black yellow
Colour is not just a colour
But coloured a different hue

You even put a different slant
On the word immigrant

You take a coloured view
And alien is not so alien
And its no lie
That immigrant whenever born
Wherever
From the New coinage
Takes on the old
Hue and cry
                        From *Black Words*

In the early 1970s I set up, with John Mapondera, Drum, a
Black arts centre to explore my 'black' identity only to discover that
I was firmly cast into the reverse side of the coin, a black trap,
defining oneself purely as 'black'. To deal with all the angst caused
by our demand for accommodation for the arts of black people and
the general frustration of black actors and activists, I became even
more stressed out and began to question if this was indeed the way
forward.

Fate, Destiny, call it what you will, came to my rescue. This
was the time of the Maharishi and Transcendental Meditation. I
decided to give it a go and it seemed that I was being guided by
forces outside myself: over the last thirty years, it has led to me to
that inner space confirming my true identity as a child of the
Universe. Also, about this same time I chanced on a copy of Aimé
Césaire's *Cahier D'un Retour Au Pays Natal* (*Notebook of a Return to
My Native Land*), which over the years has proved a blue print for
action: *Accommodate yourself to me, I won't accommodate myself to you.*
I performed it at the National Theatre in 1977 as a platform
performance and on tour for two years as a one-man show around
the country.

I had no clear idea at the time that it would lead to my
present position, that I was on a journey we all have to take at the

deepest philosophical and spiritual level, in order to return to the Source, to our Native Land – who and what we really are – that we are not separate but one with all Creation.

At the time though, its significance lay in the discovery of Africa, the dark continent of the European psyche. I discovered that Egypt was the place where the hermetic tradition of alchemy evolved, Western medicine originated and where Pythagoras, the presiding genius of the West studied for many years. I had not been aware that this would lead me to my spiritual home, to ancient African values of caring and community, thus becoming aware of the true purpose of my life.

The *Cahier* is one of the great surreal masterpieces, described by leading French Surrealist Andre Breton as 'the greatest lyrical monument of our time'. It is not only a powerful deconstruction of colonialism but an impassioned plea by the poet for an imagined return to the Africa of his forefathers, glorifying the African past and praising the traditional communal values of harmony based on intuition, caring and emotion – the 'dark senses' that seem more real than western reason and logic; a state beyond separation from Mother Earth; a desperate longing to reconnect with the 'invulnerable sap'.

But its importance has been generally misunderstood[2] – even by black intellectuals – as only extolling blackness or negritude. Wole Soyinka, famously observed that 'a tiger does not extol its tigritude.' Of course, a tiger, the epitome of environmental awareness does not have to proclaim its intrinsic nature; it is relaxed, cautious but confident, exuding grace and power in its every movement – you don't mess with a tiger! The black man has been so dehumanised and traumatised by white domination that it becomes a necessary first step for him to redefine himself, to

---

[2] Cesaire's formulation of negritude is an inclusive philosophy that draws on traditions of Africa rather than the reductionist philosophy of Leopold Senghor's group, which is largely discredited today.

rediscover his humanity, his roots in Africa where the genetic journey of the whole human race began. Asserting his blackness challenges not only his perceived place in the overall scheme of things but recuperates his own history – the greatness of ancient African civilizations like Egypt, Zimbabwe, Nubia, Ethiopia and Benin, that existed whilst Europe still slumbered in the dark ages.

Césaire's poem highlights the psychological damage caused to black people. It is a poem of great anger, matching my own at the time:

For centuries this country had proclaimed that we are brute beasts

Prima facie, it appears to be just an oppositional stance to white power, but at its deeper, more significant level, it articulates a fundamental sacredness of existence. Like the Tao, which I was soon to discover, Césaire's negritude cannot be defined, merely hinted at, as in the African Nilotic concept of total belonging; it is an animism or panpsychism of an interior awareness with infinite root that acknowledges a force vitale linking all of creation, thus giving meaning to all existence.

Because this force is positive, it is called 'vital'. It is implicit in all the pre-Christian African legends; in everything and everywhere. Animals as well as plants have it; human beings are thus always inextricably linked with each other and nature in total participation.

The *Cahier* is a plea for wholeness, a recognition of a 'blackness' which transcends race and which is quite different from that which negritude has come to mean. Césaire identified with that state of total belonging that can only be found by integrating mind and spirit, man and nature, ancient African animism and latter-day spirituality.

my negritude is not a stone
nor deafness flung out against the clamour of the day
my negritude is not a white speck of dead water
on the dead eye of the earth

There was always this feeling that I was being guided by an unknown source when I came across another book of wisdom, the *Tao Te Ching* by Lau Tzu, incomprehensible at first to someone brought up in a culture of fragmentation and duality. But as the years went by I knew that I had struck gold – Chinese alchemy – the way of nature which corresponded perfectly with African *modimo*.[3]

Initially, I was looking for another piece I could perform, in the manner of the *Cahier*. Then it was that I found a version of the *Tao Te Ching* that was much more accessible and poetic than the version I had come across just prior to immersing myself in the Cahier. Translated by the Taoist Master Gia-Fu Feng and his wife, Jane English, it seemed paradoxical and somewhat incomprehensible yet I could not put it down. I started to write down what each verse or chapter meant to me and in doing so, began creating my own 'translation'. As chance would have it, a year later, Gia-Fu Feng himself was in England giving workshops. I attended, showed him my scribblings and he was most encouraging. That same year the BBC broadcast six of my meditations on the Tao on the World Service, *The Way of Nature*, based on my paraphrase. They were repeated the following year. It seemed that at last I was on the right road.

Both Césaire and Lao Tzu talk about a sense of belonging – something that had been absent in my life and which I believe we all need in order to reassess our connection to nature. *Return to My Native Land* advocated return to nature and a value system for all

---

[3] Traditional Tswana healing is based on the concept of Modimo – an omnipotent, transcendental principle rather than a 'god'. Often translated as 'great God', modimo could not be invoked directly but only through intermediaries who received their power through revelations in a dream. Traditional healers, dismissed as 'witch doctors' by Western medicine and missionaries, have long since been recognized as 'serving vital functions of social, cultural and judicial control in the traditional society.' [The Professionalization of African Medicine' by Last and Chavunduka, 1988, p71.]

mankind which would lead to the reconciliation of opposites described in the Tao Te Ching – both texts spoke to me about wholeness.

I must confess that I do not speak Chinese. I made my paraphrase by comparing all the translations I could find and meditating on them. I found that all of the English versions differ greatly from each other, mostly, I presumed, because the Chinese who translated them may have had a limited understanding of English or that the English scholars who made their translations found the concepts difficult to comprehend.

Chinese writing is ideogramic, consisting of pictograms, which allow for a certain degree of abstraction whilst addressing themselves to the fundamental questions of existence, the nature of reality, and the mystery of creation – all of which are beyond description. Jung described the Tao as 'the undiscovered vein within us'. Indeed, the very first lines state that

The Tao that can be spoken is not the eternal Tao.

In the early 1960s I had been associated with Peter Benenson's inauguration of the human rights organisation, Amnesty International. Peter had drawn his inspiration from an ancient Chinese proverb *It is better to light a candle than to curse the darkness.* This inspired me after the frustration of Drum to set up CONCORD Multicultural festivals in the early 1980s – twenty-two inner city and two countywide programmes, celebrating the cultural diversity of Britain which, to me, reflected the diversity of nature. I felt that Britain was a microcosm of the world and could lead the way. Alas, despite their resounding success, the festivals were ignored by our media, intent it seemed on preserving the collective unconsciousness of the nation that prevails today.

In the last few months I believe that I have at last begun to understand what the purpose of my life has been about. I have written about this in my latest book, *Dark Void, Black Vision* which purports to show that Europe, in denying the roots of its own knowledge and culture has done us all the greatest possible disfavour. For Ed Mitchell, one of the last Astronauts to go to the moon, the experience of seeing our planet floating in the velvet blackness of the Dark Void was an epiphany, an ecstasy of union. He beautifully describes the interconnectedness of everything – that the 'zero point' field of energy is the starting point of all of nature's processes from which everything emanates. What he does not acknowledge is that that primordial field is none other than the Tao. Both the Tao and the latest scientific theory seem to be saying the same thing – that we have been stuck in a dualistic paradigm of division and so created a world on the brink of crisis. We need to change desperately in order to resolve the dualism that plagues our vision. We need to reconcile Heaven/Earth, Night/Day, Man/Woman, Black/White, Science/Spirituality. What in any realized completeness is an essential *duality* in absolute harmony has in the West been replaced by a *dualism,* an imbalance that results in elemental discord.

According to the Tao, opposites are but aspects of each other. Where would we be without the dark night and our dreams that connect us to the universal soul? I have written elsewhere on the reliance of traditional western science on empirical method, and the subsequent schism with anything spiritual. And I have been cheered by a 'new' physics that embraces uncertainty in a holographic vision of the universe. It is the moral imperative of what I call 'Black Vision' – outside the usual terms of black versus white – of Césaire, Fanon, Mandela, King, and latterly, Barack Obama, that will ultimately change the consciousness of mankind, who and what we really are, one with the Source, the Primordial ground of Being. It takes all the parts to make a whole and reality is more than the sum of its parts. We cannot ignore Africa, the largest continent, which I later discovered to be the home of our most recent common ancestor, the Mitochondrial Eve, described by

Césaire as the radial tree where the human race has its roots, its branches spreading out to populate our sacred planet, Earth.

As one perceptive observer notes,

> Many of us sense that we are living through a critical turning point in the evolution of consciousness. Our mechanistic ideology of manipulation and control stems from our perceived separation from nature, which is a perilous illusion. The message of cosmology, physics, biology, ecology, systems theory, mysticism and depth psychology is that we are interconnected and interdependent. We are creatures of rhythm and our fulfilment lies in harmonious relationships between ourselves and with nature. This in turn implies a new worldview,. More importantly,... the key role of blackness, darkness, the formless, the fecund void; and the dream of the dispossessed, the aspirations not only for his own people but for all mankind. The Tao contains all opposites, it is the Source and the End, the Implicate Order, the reconciliation of polarities Let us celebrate our common humanity and proclaim the advent of a new world-view rooted in ancient and perennial principles. Let us wake up from our forgetfulness, remember who we are and reclaim our true heritage of wisdom and love. [David Lorimer, from *Dark Void, Black Vision*, 2010, forthcoming]

Césaire's dream was of a new inclusive version of 'Négritude.' Martin Luther King dreamt of 'a land where men will not argue that the color of a man's skin determines the content of his character; a dream of a nation where all our gifts and resources are held not for ourselves alone, but as instruments of service for the rest of humanity; the dream of a country where every man will respect the dignity and worth of the human personality...' He declared 'that one day this nation will rise up and live out the true meaning of its creed: we hold these truths to be self-evident, that all men are created equal.'

The prevailing Western paradigm is based on a patriarchal outlook, on radical separation. According to the historian Arnold Toynbee, new cultures and worldviews emerge in response to severe challenges to society. He has been quoted as saying that 'It may be the black man who will give the new spiritual dynamic to Western civilization that it so desperately needs to survive... the spiritual power that comes from love, understanding, good will and non violence'[4]

And we are now aware of where the power of King's dream has taken us. A year later it was the voice of Nelson Mandela, from the Dock on April 20 1964. His vision of a South Africa in which all its people would have equal rights was to usher in the downfall of Apartheid and result eventually in his becoming the country's first black President. After his long incarceration, he could write in his autobiography:

> It was during those long and lonely years that my hunger for the freedom of my people became a hunger for all people, white and black. I knew as well as I knew anything that the oppressor must be liberated just as surely as the oppressed. A man who takes away another man's freedom is a prisoner of hatred, he is locked behind the bars of prejudice and narrow-mindedness. I am not truly free if I am taking away someone else's freedom, just as surely as I am not free when my freedom is taken from me. The oppressed and the oppressor alike are robbed of their humanity. When I walked out of prison, that was my mission, to liberate the oppressed and the oppressor both.
> *Long Walk to Freedom*

This vision of an integrated society was an exemplary demonstration of the power of the dream. But perhaps it was the publication of Frantz Fanon's *Black Skins, White Masks* and *The Wretched of the Earth*, which inspired the likes of King and Mandela. Like his famous teacher and mentor Aimé Césaire, he was born on Martinique. He became a psychiatrist, philosopher, revolutionary, and author and perhaps the pre-eminent black thinker of the twentieth century, his works inspiring the anti-colonial liberation

---

[4] In Stephen Oates, *Let the trumpet Sound: A life of Martin Luther King.*

movements throughout the world for more than four decades. Perhaps his greatest achievement was to describe the *mechanics*, rather than the politics of the process of colonialism.

His books were the inspiration for the Black Power movement and the struggle for civil rights in America and the root of the popular slogan *Black is Beautiful*. And the Civil Rights movement has direct links with the Women's Liberation movement. Although influenced by the Négritude Movement, Fanon formulated a new theory of consciousness which was not just about being black. Because of his recording of the role of violence in the process of national liberation, Fanon, like Césaire before him was misunderstood. The consciousness he described arises from political and social situations that affected colonized peoples of *any* racial category, and indeed apply to all bi-polar oppositions.

Fanon acknowledged his debt to Césaire whose prayer–like dream reads:

> And here at the end of the small hours is my virile prayer
> That I may hear neither laughter nor crying
> My eyes upon this city which I prophesy as beautiful.
> Give me the sorcerer's savage faith
> Give my hands the power to mould
> give my soul the temper of the sword
> I will stand firm. Make of my head a prow
> and of myself make neither a father
> nor a brother nor a son
> but the father, the brother, the son
> do not make me a husband,
> but the lover of this unique people.
>
> Make me rebellious against all vanity
> but docile to its genius...
> the time has come to gird my loins like a man of courage.
>
> But at the execution, let my heart preserve from all hate
> Do not make of me that man of hate for whom I have only hate

I was born of this unique race
But knowing my tyrannical love
you know it is not by hatred of other races that I prosecute for mine
all that I would wish
is to answer the universal hunger
the universal thirst
to prescribe at last this unique race free
to produce from its tight intimacies
the succulence of fruit.

Look. The tree of our hands is for all.

Barack Obama, the first black President of the USA said in his inauguration speech:

> This is our chance to answer that call. This is our moment. This is our time – to put our people back to work and open doors of opportunity for our kids; to restore prosperity and promote the cause of peace; to reclaim the American Dream and reaffirm that fundamental truth – that out of many, we are one; that while we breathe, we hope, and where we are met with cynicism, and doubt, and those who tell us that we can't, we will respond with that timeless creed that sums up the spirit of a people.

And what he dreams for America may help us all fulfil the power of the enduring dream if only we heeded our histories and strove to inhabit that dream.

Science, in refusing to acknowledge a spiritual dimension to creation has forced itself into a straightjacket. So have the various religions, perpetuating the division that has brought us to our present crisis. The irony is that despite this we are all part of an indivisible Whole of What is – fractals of the crystal of Creation. But still we are enmeshed in the collective unconsciousness of the prevailing worldview. When we awaken to the reality of the encompassing, compassionate Whole, thus becoming creators of our own realities we will abandon the old dualistic, fragmented paradigm that has so bedevilled our concept of who and what we really are and so usher in the New Renaissance. This is the message of the butterfly and a call to reawaken in the dream.

The Way of the TAO is Eternal.

SELECT BIBLIOGRAPHY

Bernal, Martin. *Black Athena: the Afroasiatic roots of classical civilization.* London: Free Association, 1987.

Césaire, Aimé *Cahier d'un retour au pays natal* (Return to my Native Land), trans. John Berger, Anna Bostock. Harmondsworth: Penguin, 1969.

Fanon, Frantz. *The Wretched of the Earth.* Trans. Constance Farrington; Intro. J. P. Sartre. Harmondsworth : Penguin, 1967.

Lao Tsu. *Tao te Ching,* trans Gia Fu Feng, Jane English. London: Wildwood House, 1973.

Palcy, Euzhan. *Aimé Cesaire: A Voice for History* (three-part documentary). California Newsreel, 1994.

Poe, Richard. *Black Spark, White Fire: Did African Explorers Civilize Ancient Europe?* Prima Lifestyles, 1987.

Van Sertima, Ivan. *Blacks in Science: Ancient and Modern.* New Brunswick: Transaction, 1983.